The New
Investor's
Toolbox

Using the right tools to
fine tune your financial future

FT Prentice Hall
FINANCIAL TIMES

In an increasingly competitive world, we believe it's quality of thinking that will give you the edge – an idea that opens new doors, a technique that solves a problem, or an insight that simply makes sense of it all. The more you know, the smarter and faster you can go.

That's why we work with the best minds in business and finance to bring cutting-edge thinking and best learning practice to a global market.

Under a range of leading imprints, including *Financial Times Prentice Hall*, we create world-class print publications and electronic products bringing our readers knowledge, skills and understanding which can be applied whether studying or at work.

To find out more about Pearson Education publications, or tell us about the books you'd like to find, you can visit us at **www.pearsoned.co.uk**

PEARSON
Education

The New Investor's Toolbox

Using the right tools to fine tune your financial future

HENRY HARINGTON
and ALEX HOAR

 **Prentice Hall**
FINANCIAL TIMES

An imprint of **Pearson Education**

London • New York • Toronto • Sydney • Tokyo • Singapore
Hong Kong • Cape Town • Madrid • Paris • Amsterdam • Munich • Milan

PEARSON EDUCATION LIMITED

Head Office:
Edinburgh Gate
Harlow CM20 2JE
Tel: +44 (0)1279 623623
Fax: +44 (0)1279 431059
Website: www.pearsoned.co.uk

First published in Great Britain in 2004

© Pearson Education Limited 2004

The right of Henry Harington and Alex Hoar to be identified as Authors
of this Work has been asserted by them in accordance
with the Copyright, Designs and Patents Act 1988.

ISBN 0 273 66308 9

British Library Cataloguing in Publication Data
A CIP catalogue record for this book can be obtained from the British Library.

10 9 8 7 6 5 4 3 2 1

Typeset by 70 in Palatino
Printed and bound in Great Britain by Bell & Bain Ltd, Glasgow

The Publishers' policy is to use paper manufactured from sustainable forests.

Contents

About the authors

Henry Harington, 49, has contributed to some of the world's major financial publications including *The Wall Street Journal*, the *Financial Times* and the *Banker* on the financial, banking, investment and economic issues. He served as Editor of *Equities International*, *International Financing Review* and Euromoney's *Global Investor*. He also worked as a reporter on the BBC's Money Programme. He now works as a financial writer and publishing consultant.

Alex Hoar, 34, is a trader. He spent over 12 years successfully trading on the LIFFE and London traded options markets having started his career trading commodities. He now trades on his own account and on behalf of private clients specializing in US shares, options and futures contracts. He also contributes to the financial website www.investorprofit.com and lectures at various city institutions on risk management and the derivatives markets.

Introduction

At the time of writing *The New Investor's Toolbox* retail investors, directly or through collective investment schemes like their pensions, have suffered some of the worst losses since the Great Depression. 'You can't buck the markets', there are booms and busts, always have been, and always will be. Markets tend to overshoot on the way up and overreact on the way down. Equally axiomatic is that some people will panic and others will keep their nerve.

This book is about how you, as a private investor, can learn to take control of your financial future. How you can build your wealth to prepare yourself for the uncertainties that inevitably confront us but which have been rendered all the more unpredictable by the ineptitude and deceit to which we have been subject in financial markets.

It is time for you to reclaim control of your wealth and to grow it in a way that meets your financial needs. This book is the opportunity for you to learn to look at your investments as a whole, to grow them, protect them or to enhance their performance in the way that suits your financial goals and not those of your employer, fund manager or financial adviser. *The New Investor's Toolbox* is about assessing and managing risk in simple and controlled ways, it is as much about limiting losses which can obliterate an otherwise successful investment strategy as it is about picking winners. While the book will help you determine a successful investment strategy by using the tools in the toolbox, we hope that the tools and the tactics will also cut your transactions costs. The idea is to put more money in your pocket and less in the pockets of those who secure unjustifiably large salaries and commissions in the City of London.

THE 'FREE' MARKET

When we write of 'markets' we are discussing the interrelationship of supply and demand; in the case of investments the supply of and demand for certain types of financial instrument – stocks, bonds and derivatives. The word 'market' is often prefaced by the word 'free' as in 'free markets'. We believe that the term 'free markets' is a misnomer when applied to the environment in which the retail investors hope to grow their wealth. The markets are not free; indeed this book will show they are far from free – they are very expensive!

Most of us hold a proportion of our savings not directly in stocks and bonds etc. but in collective investments like pensions and unit trusts or tax reducing 'wrappers' like Individual Savings Accounts (ISAs). In the United Kingdom these financial products are sold with little marketing flair, an absence of transparency and a lack of competition. They are sold by salesmen who have been fostered in the culture of short-termism that permeates the British financial establishment. Opaque products, like 'investment bonds' (another misnomer as they are not fixed income securities but equity-based products which give no guarantee of investors' capital being returned) are sold not on the basis of investor need but on the level of commission that will be generated. The instruments are cynically front-end loaded with charges and fees in the knowledge that inappropriate products will be abandoned by a high proportion of investors in the first few years following the purchase.

The underlying instruments in these investment products are then managed by an unimaginative coterie of risk-averse careerists. These fund managers prefer to hitch themselves to the indexation wagon so that they never have to take responsibility for the performance of the portfolios they manage; they can simply point to the index when things go wrong, shrug their shoulders and say 'it's not my fault' (Figure I.1).

In the United States there is an obligation on the part of managers of pension-based investment funds to participate in the lives of the companies in which they invest. They are required to vote at annual general meetings and take a view on corporate actions like takeovers and mergers. In Britain, the National Association of Pension Funds (NAPF) has regularly lamented the lack of participation by fund managers in the affairs of the companies they hold in trust for investors and pensioners.

The fund managers can frequently not be bothered to attend AGMs let alone participate actively in calling executives and boards to account. Indeed they are prepared to be intimidated by overbearing executives who manipulate the system of incestuous cross non-executive-directorships to burden themselves with bonuses with low trajectory targets and stock options activated solely by the inflation of stock prices.

The chart below shows how pension fund returns have plummeted.

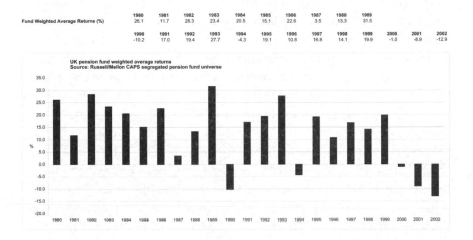

Fund Weighted Average Returns (%)	1980	1981	1982	1983	1984	1985	1986	1987	1988	1989			
	26.1	11.7	28.3	23.4	20.5	15.1	22.6	3.5	13.3	31.5			
	1990	1991	1992	1993	1994	1995	1996	1997	1998	1999	2000	2001	2002
	-10.2	17.0	19.4	27.7	-4.3	19.1	10.8	16.8	14.1	19.9	-1.0	-8.9	-12.9

Average yearly pension fund return

Figure I.1   **UK pension fund weighted average returns**
Source: Russell/Mellon CAPS segregated pension fund universe

Where there is a greater level of active management fund managers are fed a diet of 'research' by stockbrokers who seldom leave their desks to visit the companies they analyze. These 'teenage scribblers', as they were once described, are often grown men who sit at the feet of the finance directors of the companies they analyze, hanging on their every word. They rely on the figures distributed by the companies they research and which they meekly, gratefully and unquestioningly accept as scientific fact rather than the high art, alchemy and downright sophistry of the accounting profession. These 'analysts' take no initiative in seeking third-party verification or alternative sources. Moreover, this supine behaviour is encouraged by their investment bank masters who frequently have a vested interest in the advice being fed to institutions and retail investors. This has been most dramatically exposed in the United States where investment bankers have been shown to have bullied analysts into distributing 'buy' notes for shares they cynically admit, in private, are 'crap'. British investors would be naïve if they thought they were immune from such corruption.

'WHO SHALL GUARD THE GUARDIANS?'

There is another reason why British financial markets cannot be described as free: they are chained and distorted by regulation rendered impotent by subjugation to bureaucracy. Although we believe in the 'market' we do not believe that the participants in the market should be free from regulation. Every *Mirror* newspaper pensioner robbed by Robert Maxwell, every Name in the Lloyds insurance market invited unknowingly, into an asbestos syndicate, every holder of pension and endowment policies the risks of which were not explained and every misled investor in split capital trusts is an example of why investors need a guardian.

Pension mis-selling, the endowment fiasco, Equitable Life, split capital trusts, the end of final salary pension schemes, brokers (and their investment bank masters) selling investors into the 'high tech' boom which, in private, the brokers knew were 'crap', the Chinese walls between the brokerages and investment banks which proved more like Japanese paper walls, Enron, WorldCom . . . . And that's just the 1990s.

Go back a little further and we have the Third World debt crisis, the savings and loans debacle, the high leveraged bond (junk bond) disasters . . . the list goes on.

We believe passionately that responsibility for the financial wreckage chronicled in the paragraphs above can be placed firmly at the doors of financial advisors, financial regulators and the government.

There are several areas of blame: the creation of a regulatory regime which allowed failed second-hand car salesmen to sell financial products, the perpetuation of the illusion that the state will provide, and above all the failure to educate the investing public about how to grow and protect their wealth.

Banking and financial services have not covered themselves in glory in the past couple of decades. They have not done a particularly good job for their shareholders and they have skinned those buying their products leaving them feeling raw, exposed and vulnerable. The regulatory industry has reacted with the speed and decisiveness of a blind night watchman – seeking absolution by accumulating restrictions, adding more warnings and printing more brochures and of course, tut-tutting.

In the UK the number of people who have gone to prison for major frauds against investors since the introduction of the Financial Services

Act in 1986 can be counted on the fingers of one hand. Anyone who has lodged a complaint with the Financial Services Authority or the Financial Services Ombudsman will have needed the persistence and patience of a condemned man going through the American appeal process.

So ineffective was the regime of 'old school tie' self-regulation that it became an embarrassment. The system was abandoned and a new regulatory empire was created in a glistening tower in Canary Wharf. This edifice is a factory for the generation of inefficiency and red tape. There seems to be more interest in the annexation of new areas to regulate than, for example, highlighting the risks of Equitable Life or passing on the warnings from the Guernsey regulator of the dangers of split capital trusts.

Love them or hate them we all need financial markets – money *does* make the world go around, look how slow it can get when there is no money in your pocket.

The nanny world of the Financial Services Authority insists on rambling warnings – investors aren't stupid, they know 'the value of investments goes up and down and that past performance is no indication of the future'. And yet, great swathes of the investing public have been afflicted by some form of financial ineptitude or mis-selling. So how have investors got themselves in this pickle?

In a word 'trust'. They trusted the august financial institutions and they trusted the regulators to punish those who transgressed. In recent years governments have utilized the phrase 'welfare dependency' to describe those people for whom it is easier to collect social benefits than find a job.

Investors have succumbed to 'advice dependency' because they believe financial advisers can do better than they can. Many are now paying the price.

Part of what we see as the failure of the financial services industry is its unwillingness to embrace the tools described in this book. If you call your broker today and ask him to put a stop loss order on a share purchase he will tell you it can't be done. It can be done, but British brokers are unwilling to invest in the software that will allow them to offer this service.

If you believe the market is set for a fall and you ask your broker about buying a put option to protect your portfolio, the chances are he will suck through his teeth and tell you 'don't go there'. When you ask why he will lecture you on the dangers of derivatives but the real reason is that he does not understand them.

In being unable to offer you these tools your broker is failing you. The tools discussed in this book help you to take a holistic approach to your investments, by ignoring them the broker is like a garage that puts petrol in your tank but does not put oil in the engine or air in the tyres.

FINANCIAL EDUCATION

In this book we argue that much of the energy devoted to regulation would, in the long term (not a phrase with which the City is familiar or comfortable), be better expended on financial education and which would lead to a new regime of personal self-regulation. Not self-regulation by the phalanxes of 'Self-Regulatory Organisations' (SROs) which previously failed investors and had to be replaced by the new superstructure of the Financial Services Authority (FSA). The future of investor security is in self-regulation through education.

Financial education has been an 'hurrah' term in the past couple of years. Every time there is a financial scandal the Prime Minister, the Treasury, the FSA, the Association of British Insurers and all the reports that are commissioned come to the same conclusion: 'Financial education (like motherhood and apple pie) is a "good thing"'. But that is as far as it gets. No one has a battle plan; there is no constituency in the provision of financial education. Despite the large number of voters whose financial security is being undermined by ignorance about financial markets it has yet to become a live issue.

And the market practitioners are in the role of the Church in the Middle Ages. The Church did not want the Bible to be translated from Latin into English because it would have empowered parishioners to question the mystery of God and, heaven forbid, even have a direct line to the Godhead thus bypassing the vicarage, archbishopric and the Pope. God forbid the retail investor should understand the mysteries of the financial markets!

There is currently no proper provision in the National Curriculum for financial education. Students leave schools and colleges with certificates confirming they have competency in anything from bricklaying to history to media studies. But they have no idea where to cash their first wage cheque, why not to use store-card credit cards, how to invest in a pension, which mortgage would suit their requirements when they come to buy a house and have received no guidance whatsoever as to where to procure this information. The analogy of lambs being released into a world full of hungry wolves does not overstate the dangers these unsuspecting financial novices face.

WHO SHOULD READ THE NEW INVESTOR'S TOOLBOX?

While we believe that there is a great shortcoming in the educational system this book is not aimed at the financially uninitiated.

You are probably someone who already has some investments or savings. You will probably be buying a house on a mortgage, have a pension linked to your employment and, perhaps, a private pension. You already have an interest in investing and have relied to date on a financial adviser or a broker.

But crucially you want greater understanding and independence either to manage your investments yourself or to be able to operate on a level playing field with your broker or financial adviser.

The primary purpose of *The New Investor's Toolbox* is to describe and educate investors about the exciting and innovative tools that can be used to help them protect and generate wealth. However, the book is not simply descriptive; we also discuss the strategies investors can use to get the best out of their portfolios. Indeed we would like to see the book as a manual to which readers refer again and again as the markets or their circumstances throw up new conditions to which different tools or strategies can be applied.

But in offering access to *The New Investor's Toolbox* we feel it is vital to indicate why we think that investors should use the tools and strategies and why to 'buy and hold' will be a flawed strategy for anyone hoping to accumulate and protect their wealth.

This introduction provides an analysis of how retail investors have been abused by bureaucratic regulators and financial advice that borders on, and sometimes falls over, into the criminal. We do not want to labour the self-serving of the regulators and financial advisers. However, we feel that by highlighting their deficiencies, the excessive commissions, the hidden charges and the opacity of management fees that we will give the readers of *The New Investor's Toolbox* the justification for finding their own way and learning to manage their own wealth creation.

Winston Churchill in appealing to the Americans for the wherewithal to tackle the Germans said: 'Give us the tools and we will finish the job'. Our aim in this book is to equip investors to manage and fine-tune their investment portfolios. The book's main aim is to describe a box of financial tools that investors can use to access the independence of financial advice or to be able to speak to financial advisers on their own terms. Crucially the book is not just about defining the fascinating tools that are now available to the retail investor. It is an explanation of how to use the tools; the strategy and tactics that will help you reach your financial goals.

THE TOOLS

Over the past 20 years computers and telecommunications have been developing and converging, with futurologists claiming this technology is going to change our lives. A generation ago an IBM mainframe computer filled a house, cost a mint and caused the nation's lights to dim as it added 2 and 2. Today we have greater computing power in a desktop computer, we can access the Internet and computer chips facilitate almost every aspect of our lives.

To much less acclaim the boffins in the world's financial centres, often called 'rocket scientists', have been developing instruments and strategies to help big investors like insurance companies and pension funds to better manage their money – our money.

For most people the only insight into this arcane world was the periodic implosions that ripped through the financial laboratories of the rocket scientists when they added the wrong ingredients. The newspapers sagely informed us of the high-octane fuels being used in financial markets and how dangerous they were. The catastrophic collapse of Barings Bank is usually cited as a Frankenstein's monster being created by the lunatics in some financial Transylvania.

We would not have written this book if we believed that these instruments were dangerous. We reject any suggestion that Barings and other financial disasters should be laid at the doors of the tools covered in this book. There is ample evidence that behind the headlines blaming the tools it was the workmen and their managers who were in fact to blame. It has been failures of management and dishonesty rather than any inherent dangers of these instruments. The biggest failure of all has been the incompetence of senior managers who did not take the trouble to understand the instruments, failed to make proper risk assessment and were blinded by greed fed by the deceit of their subordinates.

It suited the regulators and the financial institutions alike to blame derivatives, in the same way as aeroplane manufacturers always pray crashes of their planes can be attributed to pilot error rather than any failing on the part of their aeroplanes.

In pillorying managers of organizations like Barings and the Supervision Committee of the Bank of England (which produced a worthy report on the Barings collapse without bothering to speak to its instigator, Nick Leeson), we are not saying the tools in *The New Investor's Toolbox* are without risk. As part of the discussion of strategy in each chapter we discuss what can go wrong and how to avoid things going pear-shaped.

Also, we do not expect the managers of financial institutions or you to understand the rocket science underlying the tools – you don't have to know how crude oil is made into petrol to drive a car. But you do have to understand that if you put your foot down on the accelerator you go faster and become more of a danger than by sitting with the engine idling.

By understanding the capacity and the limits of the tools you understand the risks and the potential rewards. This book is not a recipe for 'getting rich quick'. Our aim is to better equip you to invest and manage your money successfully and to understand and minimize risk (not avoid risk, as without risk there is no return). In the process we will show you how you can trade in a more cost-effective way by using different tools, strategies and investment vehicles.

As we will discuss, managing your money does not necessarily mean making more money by buying low and selling high. It can mean making fewer losses, it can mean protecting money from the vicissitudes of the market, and it can mean fine tuning a portfolio to increase returns by optimizing risks. Everyone who has investments has a different reason for saving and needs a different set of tools and strategies to achieve their goals.

We hope that by reading this book investors will understand the tools and see how they can use them to improve their own financial lives.

FAREWELL WELFARE

If the tools in *The New Investor's Toolbox* don't convince you of their value on their own merits, if you are still sceptical about the culpability of the regulatory and financial services industry in the destruction of wealth and sleight of hand over charges and delivery, then we think the following scenario will convince you that you need to take your financial affairs in hand to protect yourself and your family.

The welfare state is legalized fraud and as deceitful as any Ponzi scam or pyramid scheme. That is not to detract from the concept and the benefits that most of us have enjoyed since we have lived in the hey day of the welfare state with education, health care, subsidized prescriptions, unemployment benefit and, until the last few years, eye care and dentistry.

But if something sounds too good to be true it almost certainly is and the welfare state is unsustainable. 'That does not make it a fraud' we hear you say: the illusion is created that we bear the pain of tax today to insure ourselves against the uncertainties of tomorrow – unemployment, illness, old age and long-term care.

The fraud is that our taxes and national insurance contributions were not taken from us and invested, there was no fund created and built up for all our rainy days. It was not like paying an insurance premium to an insurance company which invests the money and compensates you when your house burns down or you have a burglary.

Our taxes and National Insurance contributions went in the front door of HM Treasury and straight out the back door. It was spent willy-nilly by successive governments to pay for current spending on health and welfare.

You may not agree that it is a deceit to extract money from people today to pay for their future pensions and simply give it to those who are receiving a pension today. You may say that provided the welfare benefits going out of the Treasury are matched by the money rolling into the Inland Revenue that you will not lose any sleep. Our advice is to go out now and buy some sleeping pills! If you or your children are under 40 then when you or they get to the state pension cupboard it will be bare. Even those over 40 know that if you want an eye test, prescription or need to see a consultant that there is a cost or a delay because the money is already being rationed.

The UK Government's proposal for a Child Trust Fund (the 'Baby Bond') under which every child reaching the age of 18 will be funded to kick-start a private pension is an admission that a cradle-to-grave welfare state is over.

Britain, like most developed countries, is facing a demographic time bomb. The post-Second World War 'baby boom' population is ageing into a 'grey bulge'. Ironically the fruits of the welfare state (better food, better education, better health care) are ensuring that these people live longer. But as things stand, they are not working longer and not paying tax longer. Indeed, many of the elderly will spend a greater proportion of their lives as pensioners than they did working. Even plans to increase the retirement age to 70 are not going to mature the problem out of the way.

People are living longer (Figure I.2). Great. Yes, it is great in the fantasy world of grey-haired people on Golden Pond enjoying a happy, healthy and prosperous retirement. If only life were really like that. The fact is that people who live longer draw pensions longer, pensions being paid by current taxpayers. People who live longer place increasing demands on the health and social services. Medical advances are helping to keep people alive and mobile for longer but new procedures and medicines are expensive. And finally, when the elderly become infirm they need long-term care, and because the welfare state made them a healthy bunch, they will need long-term care longer.

In the great scheme of things none of this matters. By the year 2100 there will not be many baby boomers knocking around. Indeed, today's sexually active generation are marrying later (if they marry). They are more likely to have fewer children than their parents or will have no children at all because they concentrate on careers and forego children or are gay, something members of the older generation may have hidden, having children despite themselves.

Already the UK's birth rate has fallen to an all time low of 1.6 children per woman against the 2.1 required simply to replace the dying. The combined effects of a declining birth rate and ageing population mean that in 2005 the European population will have peaked at 305 million. By 2015 one in five of its population will be over 65 years of age, by 2050 one third of Europeans will be over pensionable age (*Financial Times*, 13 May 2002).

There is the prospect of an inverted pyramid of a small workforce (representing a shrunken tax base) supporting a burgeoning demand for health care, pensions and long-term care. These obligations are set to overwhelm the financial capacity of even the best intentioned of governments.

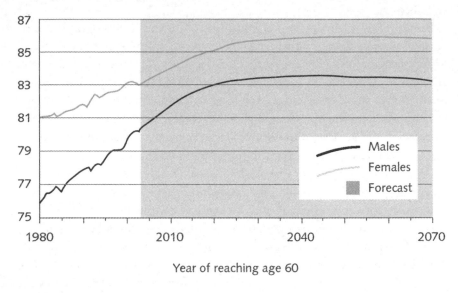

Average life expectancy at 60

Year of reaching age 60

Figure I.2   **Ageing UK**
Source: Government Actuary's Department

The short-term electoral imperative means politicians have ducked the issue and there has been a signal failure on the part of governments to confront this very long-term problem. There has been an 'after me the flood' conspiracy of deceit about state 'funding' – pensions and health schemes are not 'funded' but pay-as-you-go, paid for out of current tax revenues. There is no 'National Insurance Fund', no reserve tank. The vision for former prime minister, John Major, of the deafening sound of wealth cascading from generation to generation will be replaced by a great sucking sound as savings and home equity disappear into the void of support for an old and infirm population.

PENSION PENURY

Many have become alert to the failure of the pensions industry by the painful medium of experience. More will face these realities as the full force of declining stock market returns, falling annuity rates, the erosion of the state pension and the jettisoning of final salary pension schemes become all too painfully evident (Figure I.3).

The National Association of Pension Funds (NAPF) published its annual survey in December 2002 and the following are some of its key, and very disturbing, findings:

- Eighty-four guaranteed or final-salary schemes were closed in 2002, almost double the rate in 2001.
- Employer contributions into replacement money-purchase schemes are running at less than half the level of final-salary schemes.
- A typical employee in a money-purchase scheme is £100 a month worse off than their counterpart in a final-salary scheme.
- Thirty per cent of private–employer schemes are now closed to new entrants compared with 17 per cent in 2001 and 12 per cent in 2000.

But many of us are living with denial and ignoring the extent to which we will be dependent on the state in our retirement (Figure I.4).

% of average earnings

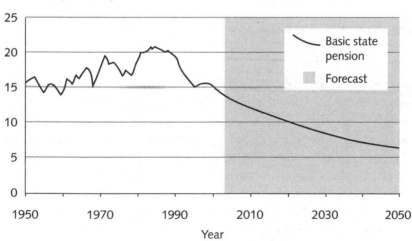

Basic state pension to men on average earnings, expressed as a percentage of average earnings, and increasing in line with prices

Figure I.3   **Value of basic pension falls**
Source: Government Actuary's Department

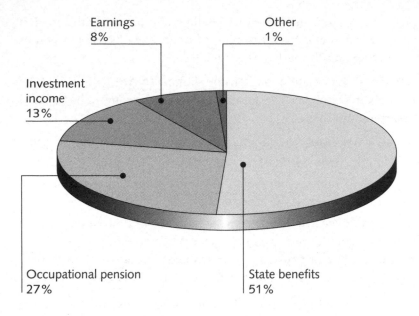

Sources of gross income of pensioner households, 2000/1

Figure I.4   **Pensioners' incomes**
Source: Department for Work and Pensions

Equitable Life has robbed many honest, law-abiding savers of the prospect of a comfortable retirement. The 'advice dependency' has meant for many of us abrogating responsibility for our financial futures to actuaries and pension plans run by our employers, or even by ourselves, handing over our pension contributions directly to a pensions company. The pension plans have not performed. Our employers (legitimately) skimmed off the cream in times of surplus and now that the managers they chose have failed to deliver are casting their employees adrift. Gone are the comfortable final-salary schemes with which employers bribed you into their employ. In their place are the defined-contribution schemes that expose you to all the uncertainties of the marketplace.

For those who have taken their pensions in the last couple of years or are seeking an annuity the news is disastrous (Figure I.5). You, the individual private investor, are threatened by the demographic dam that is about to overflow. You need to plan, build and protect your financial

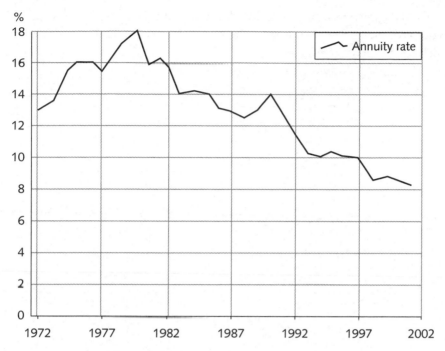

Average returns for people who turn their retirement lump sum into an annual income

Figure I.5 **How annuity rates have fallen**

Source: Cannon and Tonks (2000). CMPO paper 02/051. University of Bristol

future. Your first port of call should be a financial adviser, broker, pension company, investment manager – someone you can trust with your future.

But with the lamentable record of the financial services industry over the past few years you are cast on your own resources. At school you learned the name of the capital city of Russia and how William the Conqueror invaded England in 1066. You didn't learn what a share was, how a company operates, why profits are made, how a pension works and why we all need to save and manage our finances.

We make no claim in this book that you could manage your financial affairs better than a financial adviser, we just think that armed with the knowledge in this book we would be very surprised if you did worse! Or, if you plan to use a financial adviser, this book will put you on a level playing field.

Unlike your financial adviser we don't just take your money and run. If you have questions arising from the book please contact us by e-mail at tools@investorprofit.com .

1

Understanding risk

DIVING UNDER THE DUVET

Even refusing to get out of bed in the morning because you are concerned about the day's risks is risky (your house could be struck by a meteorite, the duvet might spontaneously combust, your partner may leave you because you have no drive . . .).

But you have to learn to balance life's everyday risks against the rewards on offer, and it's no different when committing capital to the markets. Trading and investing is about accepting risk, taking on risk with the aim of making a reward. Simply put, trading and investing is about the risk/reward ratio. For every potential associated risk there is a potential associated reward connected to it, and if either the risk or the potential reward is not acceptable then it's normally not a good trade or investment to make.

This is the main point that many people miss when dealing in the markets. They think trading or investing is just about making money. Of course, money or seeing one's account appreciate must be the ultimate goal but in reality trading is more about being aware of, interpreting and analyzing risk than making a reward. This means questions about both risk and reward have to be asked before a trade or account is put into action. And as you can see in Figure 1.1, the higher the rate of return that you require, the higher the amount of risk you're going to have to assume. This point is fundamental across the whole spectrum of trading and investing, whoever you are, whatever your investment goals and whatever the size of your account.

THE IMPORTANCE OF FOUNDATIONS

Every good business is built on firm principles and foundations. A trading plan or investment strategy built along these lines is one that will not only last, but will generate the necessary confidence and ability to trade through both the good and bad times – and even the best market participants have some bad times, their secret is not to lose heart or lose nerve.

We believe there are four basic foundations to successful trading and investment:

1   A good understanding of what you're doing and the products you're going to use.
2   Understanding the risk/reward ratio.
3   Keeping your trading simple and using common sense.
4   Keeping costs low.

If you want to make money in the markets then you must start to build and formulate your own ideas and foundations because, ultimately, successful trading is like any other business – there has to be plan. Think of any well-run company. It might be a small firm of electricians or perhaps a multinational soft drink manufacturer, but whatever the size it will be run and operated with some sort of business plan and set of foundations to follow. Many traders today don't look at trading this way, they open an account and then buy and sell usually on a whim, or using someone's else's advice and then wonder why it often goes wrong.

Start to think of your trading capital like an engine on a ship. You want the engine to operate on the most efficient cost basis possible. If you put in too much fuel (risk) then the engine could blow up, if too little then you won't get anywhere. Some traders like owning speedboats and they're the ones who (if they are right) get all the glory, but crash and burn if they get it wrong. Others prefer the slow stable power of a tug, and while they'll never be the stars of the harbour they're likely to remain in business for many years. Choose your boat and engine, formulate some plans and then you'll start to approach the game of trading and investment as the professionals do.

Foundation 1 – Understand what you're doing and the products you're going to be using

As strange as this may seem, many people with trading accounts do not know what they're doing, especially in today's fast-paced markets. They lose money for the most foolish reasons and often never know exactly why. Making money over time in the markets is not the easiest of endeavours and that is why if you play the game without setting yourself up with the correct knowledge, you will make it so much harder on yourself.

Utilizing traded options is a good example of this. In the wrong hands and without the necessary skill and knowledge, options are often a quick way to lose money, or perhaps an efficient tool for transferring money from the people who don't fully understand them to people who do! It is easy to be enthused or carried away by an exciting two-page article in a magazine saying how options can make you good money. But the article due to obvious space restraints can only scratch the surface of these often complex financial tools. So when a trader new to options gets disastrous results it will often be because they simply didn't fully understand what they were doing, rather than their overall call on market direction. So if you're contemplating using options then make sure you do your homework beforehand as it will often save you big money in the future.

The good news, however, is that you don't have to do a lot of work in order to understand how to use products such as options, but you must do more than the majority of new traders or investors. Look at your education as a twofold process. First, thoroughly investigate the theory and inner workings behind the products and this information can be found very easily these days via books such as this or the Internet, where a lot of information is free. Be wary, though, with this information because textbook theory in the financial markets is often very different from the application in real-time markets. The second part of your education should be in trading the products and it is always wise to start off as small as you can. You may have a very large account but you'll soon find out that the markets care little about how well capitalized you are. It is as easy these days to lose £1,000 as £100,000.

The learning process via books or other printed / online material should be your foundation but the real-time trading is where the all important experience is built up. Think of it as being similar to a well-trained soldier, he may have had the best training that money can buy, but a soldier with the same training combined with battlefield experience is much more valuable. On the battlefield there is real danger, and so in the markets although blood does not spill from wounds, capital is as precious a resource.

The other important part about trading in real-time markets is the fact that most good traders and investors tend to learn from mistakes, mistakes that are never made in the so-called classroom. In fact, losses, as painful and uncomfortable as they are, often can be viewed simply as the price one pays for education. However, you must learn from them and while it is impossible to entirely eliminate mistakes from your trading, the better traders and investors are, by definition, the ones who normally make fewer mistakes. The authors know one very good trader in particular who makes this his *modus operandi* in that his development in the business has been characterized by making fewer and fewer mistakes every year. So that his continuing improving results over the years arise directly from this approach and not by buying and selling in the market at more advantageous prices or getting more winning trades in his account.

The other important point about the education process that you must realize is that you only have to know about the products in the way in which you wish to apply them. For example, with traded options there are three main uses, speculation, hedging and income generation. If you're interested in using them for hedging purposes and not speculation then concentrate all your efforts where they'll be best served.

Foundation 2 – The risk/reward ratio

People are drawn into financial markets by the potential rewards. But that is only half of the equation.

A famous trader once stated that he followed only two rules in his business:

1   If you don't trade you can't win.
2   If you lose all your money you can't trade.

These rules simply mean that you have to risk money in order to make money, but if you risk too much and those risks don't pay off, then you'll lose the potential to make money in the future. And don't laugh at the obvious statement 'you have to risk money to make money' because many people in the markets don't even consider the risk aspect, they buy a stock because it will make them money if and when it goes up. The potential risk that buying this stock entails never enters their mind until events are visited upon them, and, of course, once in a losing position further problems always materialize. Should they wait and see what happens, hope the stock will rally back up, buy some more to average down etc? These are questions that all good traders try to find answers to before the event.

To be a good trader you must get a good grip and understanding of the risk/reward ratio and you should realize that risk is always far more important than reward. In order to be a successful investor over time, capital preservation *must* become your number one priority, with capital appreciation coming a close second.

But what is the 'risk/reward ratio'? Simply put it is the amount of money a trader is willing to risk in order to make an expected return. And, however obvious this may sound, you want to be looking for trades that offer more profit potential than loss. Many professional traders like to find trades with the ratio of 3:1 in mind, or risking £1 to make £3. If you can find trades or investments with this sort of profile then even if your trading ideas are only 50 per cent right your account will still generate excellent returns.

Understanding the risk/reward ratio

Figure 1.1 illustrates the risk/reward ratio – study and understand!

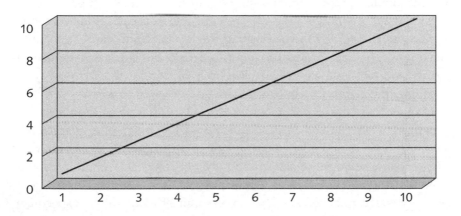

Figure 1.1 Risk and reward – where do you stand?

What's your risk/reward ratio?

Figure 1.1 shows that the amount of reward one seeks has a direct relationship with the amount of risk that has to be assumed. If you have ambitions of making large returns on your capital, be prepared for large potential drawdowns as well. A drawdown is the percentage move lower that an account suffers from an associated equity level. An account of £100k that is reduced to £60k has suffered a 40 per cent drawdown.

The banking industry is a pretty good example of how this risk/reward ratio works in the markets. Citicorp may offer to pay you 2 per cent on your US dollar deposits while an Argentinean bank offers far more. Why? Citicorp is a US owned and regulated bank whose accounting system is transparent and which is being monitored by depositors, regulators, rating agencies and analysts on a continuous basis for any sign of trouble. It is also based in the stable and secure US of A. The Argentinean bank is based in, well, Argentina which has been having a rocky economic time of late, there have been currency crises, runs on its banks and fears of national bankruptcy. Yes, you can place your deposit in the Argentinean bank and, yes, you can earn a far higher rate of interest. But can you live with the sleepless nights of not knowing if the bank or the country's economy will disappear off the radar screen! There is obviously a much higher risk premium associated with the Argentinean bank and if you deposit your money there you'll be entitled to a greater reward. But how many of us are blinded by the double-digit interest rate and how many of us spell out to ourselves the risk inherent in earning these rates?

Of course, in following the risk/reward line in the diagram everyone would prefer it to be drawn nearer to the top left-hand corner, meaning maximum potential profits for minimum risk. But the markets deal in reality and facts, and whatever your style of trading there's no way of escaping the relationship between risk and reward over time.

In order to decide what risk/reward profile your trading should follow you need to ask yourself a simple question. 'How much of my capital am I willing to risk?', and not just on any one trade but over a series of trades. Don't follow what most new traders do and only ask questions about potential rewards, try and look at both sides of the trading equation. If you are very well capitalized and have excess money with which to speculate then perhaps you'll be comfortable taking on large risks and therefore your account could be expected to make large returns if your investment strategies work. That would place you in the top right-hand corner of the graph. But if your goal is capital preservation then you should be located towards the bottom left-hand corner of the graph and your potential returns will reflect this.

However important the amount of money they make for their clients (and it is important), most money managers are judged by their risk-adjusted returns rather than just the money that they make. Someone new to investing would always assume that a trader who made 200 per cent in a year is streets ahead of one that only made a 15 per cent return on capital invested. But this is not always the case because you have to look at how much money each trader risked in order to make their respective returns. You will often find that the best traders are normally those who make slightly above average gains but do so with very little risk or drawdown to their funds.

Chase profit, ignore the risks at your peril

A classic example of what happens when you don't either respect the risk in the markets or simply disregard it was demonstrated by the great dotcom boom of the late 1990s. Rumour became fact, fact became law and the belief held sway for a while that financial markets could defy not only the old measures of stock valuation but gravity itself. The majority of people who lost money by playing with technology stocks did so because they only thought about one thing, how much money they could make. The evidence that these people did not give a moment's notice to risk came in the smell of burned fingers which was hanging over the market long after the dotcoms had bombed.

These dotcom stocks carried not only unbelievable profit potential but also, as Figure 1.1 implies, maximum risk. Think about it logically: any stock or market that has the potential to move violently one way, also has the potential to move in the other direction. But many buyers of the technology stocks didn't realize the risks that they were carrying until it was too late. Of course, it's easy to be wise after the event, but this example simply seeks to highlight the danger of being blinded by profits and making money. The potential of mega profits in any stock or market therefore must always be measured by the risks involved.

Risk is ultimately more important than reward

Trading and investing is a game where you can enjoy success over many years only to lose it all in a matter of weeks or months. The trading community is littered with such cases. This is why risk is far more important than reward. Making money will never really give an investor sleepless nights or undue worry, but losing money can force one to make dangerous decisions such as doubling up or trying to play catch-up with your losses.

In order to be a good trader you should get into the practice of always starting with your risk analysis and then looking at the potential rewards available, not the other way around. Don't worry about how much money you'll make; always think about potential losses, how much can you afford to lose and at what level you should take the losses, etc. Before every trade get into the habit of asking yourself how much money you're willing to risk, then and only then should you look at the potential rewards on offer. In fact many good traders make it their policy to pass on certain trades even if the profit potential looks attractive because they can't or are unwilling to accept the risk that would have to be assumed. An example of this would be a trader who feels that the FTSE 100 has a good chance of rising over 100 points in a day, but for whatever reason would have to use a 50 point stop loss. His view is that it's uneconomical to risk 50 points in order to make 100, but, of course, decisions such as this always vary from trader to trader.

Foundation 3 – Keeping your trading simple and using common sense

It's a fact of trading and investing that for most people the simple strategies work best. Think about it. If brains and computer power were the passports to success then the investment banks and their legions of traders, analysts, strategists and the like would literally own the world. They have all the computer power you could ask for and all the rocket scientists to package intricate and convoluted deals. But take a look at their results from proprietary trading over the years, and you'll find that they are as haphazard as the markets themselves.

It has been said of common sense that it should be called 'rare sense' because there is so little of it about. Common sense should be ubiquitous in your trading. But what is common sense in the marketplace? Not throwing good money after bad by doubling down on a stock in order to reduce your average price (unless this is part of your trading plan); not getting too greedy; being disciplined when taking profits and losses; using stop losses (discussed in Chapter 4); not trading in products you don't fully understand; not trading short term when you can't follow the markets, etc. Common sense should be obvious when trading and investing and if you ever find yourself trying to be too clever then this is often a warning sign as to future losses.

Foundation 4 – Keeping costs low

Trading, as you'll see many times in this book, is simply like any business, and all businesses have costs, whether fixed or variable. The two main costs in trading and investment are commissions and the bid–offer spread, and it's almost certain that many readers of this book are overpaying in commissions. With the boom days of the late 1990s over its been a buyers' market for client commissions since the year 2000. Not only that, many brokerage clients have suffered losses so there is generally less business to go around which should make the brokers hungrier for their business. All traders should look very closely at what they're paying for in relation to what other brokers are offering. For too long the average retail client has been hoodwinked by his broker when it comes to charges.

Why is the cost of commissions so important? Because it comes straight off the bottom line. If you're paying an average of £3,000 of costs a year and reduce this to £1,500 then the difference is pure profit without you having to do anything different in the marketplace. But one of the main problems with commissions is that on any one trade they might not seem to be a problem, but even a saving of 0.1 per cent on every stock deal can add up significantly over the course of the year. In Chapter 5 on Contracts for Differences (CFDs) we'll look into commissions in more detail and readers will probably be surprised at just how much damage different rates can cause over the long run.

Bid–offer spreads can also be a significant cost in doing business. It's not uncommon for the difference in price between the bid–offer spread on some smaller stocks and option contracts to be as wide as 10–15 per cent. Trading products such as these can cause almost insurmountable odds against the trader because the costs will be added to any loss and taken away from any profit. If the bid–offer is 5 per cent then you need to make at least 5 per cent just to break even. Try not to get involved in products where you can't get inside the bid–offer by quoting your own price. You will see further examples of this is Chapter 6 on traded options where although the bid–offers are often very wide the trader always has the prerogative to tighten them up. For example, if the market on an XYZ call option is 110–120 and you wish to buy then you can bid the market, say, 115. But with some small market-maker stocks traded in London the only prices that you can deal on is the market-maker quote. Unless you can control the bid–offer yourself it's often good advice to leave these kind of stocks alone, unless you're going to be a longer-term investor in which case it doesn't matter so much because your expected profits should go a long way to overcoming the costs involved.

The cost of business also includes other expenses such as computers and data feeds. Many traders like to have the best equipment combined with an efficient price feed but with the advent of the web, combined with a fast Internet connection, a good deal of information that cost a bomb a few years ago is now either free or has been reduced in price dramatically. Try to look at the equipment that you buy or use on a rate-of-return basis. If you're spending over £1,000 a month on your data feeds, etc. then you should, on average, be expecting to make far more than that. Most traders and investors do not need to spend a lot of money and these days it's possible to have a good computer, Internet connection and real-time prices for under £50 a month, which is incredibly good value as a few years ago similar services would have cost nearer £500.

COMMITTING YOURSELF

That is not an instruction for you to be come more dedicated in your investment but to commit your ideas to paper. Understanding risk and your capacity to adopt it will be all the clearer if you write down what your objectives are and how you want to achieve them. We suggest you do this for an overall approach to your investments, outlining your goals, what you would like to achieve and broadly how you would like to meet your investment goals. But committing yourself to paper does not end there: you should write down what your strategy is each time you plan a transaction; what you hope to achieve, how you hope to achieve it, what you expect the return to be, what you expect the costs to be.

Like a photographer who writes down the film speed, the aperture, the shutter speed, the light conditions, time of day, what filters he used, etc. you will find that you go back to your notes time and time again. Either you will return because you want to make sure you don't make that mistake again or, more pleasurably, you will return to find the recipe for that 'magic formula' for the trades that really worked for you.

There is nothing complicated in stating your objectives to yourself and nor are they set in stone – circumstances beyond your control may well alter how you perceive things. But expressing yourself and even sleeping on your plans can really help to clarify your objectives. How many of us have wished we had slept on that rude letter we sent to someone and would have torn it up and written a more reasoned missive had we slept on it? The same applies to your investment plans.

Here is an example of expressing investment goals.

Example

John Smith – Investment Goals

I am a forty-one-year-old administrator working for a multinational retail company. I have a company pension which has been changed from a final-salary scheme that would have given me a pension of around two-thirds of my final salary. I am not banking on the defined-contribution scheme giving me any more than half my final salary. I have a mortgage on my house that will be paid off by the time I retire. I have £35,000 in investments. I have opted for a pretty conservative investment strategy in my company pension scheme: my contributions are being put into bonds and blue chip shares, main indexes like the FTSE 100.
Returns on shares are around 2 per cent p.a. at present. I want to increase the growth on my portfolio to 7 per cent p.a.

I plan to put one half into exchange-traded funds for a core portfolio to spread some of the risk. This will be a low-risk form of investing. I'll look to put a quarter into covered warrants focused on the retail sector because this is an area I understand. And the final quarter will be my high-risk portfolio and I'll use a range of tools as and when I identify specific opportunities. I won't expose myself in any individual transaction and I will always define my risk before any trade using stop losses where possible. I understand the risks and products that I'll be trading in and realize that experience is the best teacher, so to be prudent to start with I will make sure that my trades are small by nature, however bullish or bearish I may feel.

The sources on information I will use will be the *Investor's Chronicle*, ADFN.com, and the weekend *FT*. I will monitor the charts from Metastock.
I will not expect to pay more than £x In brokerage and fees and I will try and use instruments offer competitive rates to deal in as well as reasonably tight bid–offer spreads.

I will monitor my trading portfolio on a daily basis but will try to stand back and look at the bigger picture for my investment trades.

➔ summary

Many people often wonder why trading, investing and increasing one's capital is so hard in financial markets? The truth is it's normally the trader who is at fault not his ability to pick the right shares or market direction. The authors have a lot of experience with retail clients and without doubt they make it hard for themselves by not following the four foundation rules listed above. The authors' own trading is far from perfect and when we trace back problems in our trading they will always be in someway related to one or more of the foundations.

Normally we find the problem is related to Foundation 3, common sense. Try and get too clever in the market whoever you are, and you'll often find that losses or missed opportunities are often your only reward.

We readily admit that while the four foundations are simple enough to state, they are a lot harder to practice in real-time trading, apart from Foundation 4, reducing costs. Is one foundation more important than another in the overall context of trading? No, they all feed and are connected to each other but traders would be well advised to pay particular attention to the risk/reward ratio, for far too much money is lost by people not respecting risk which is the dominant factor in every trade or investment. In fact, even if your trading ideas are lousy, if you respect the risk and take manageable losses you will probably do far better than a trader with excellent trading ideas who neglects this topic.

Time is also an important element in trading and investing for it offers the all-important experience. Many people think even if they are successful in another business field they can simply translate this success into trading profits. But this is not so. Imagine if you were a successful lawyer who changed careers to deal in property. Would you instantly be able to make a success of this venture or would your new career be plagued by unforeseen problems? Perhaps after a few years in property your new career would be sufficiently endowed with the necessary experience and knowledge to make it a solid financial success. It's no different in trading and investing.

2

Short selling

IT'S NOT CRICKET

You are watching a cricket match with a friend from India. He boldly states that he fancies his Indian compatriots will score at least 400 runs. You disagree and so decide to have a bet. You wager £20 on the fact that India will not make 400 runs during their innings, therefore if the Indians score under 400 you'll win £20 from your friend. If India scores over 400 runs you will lose £20.

ADDING MORE SPICE TO THE WAGER

In the financial markets deals are never executed for a fixed wager as in the example above. So let's expand on the cricket bet.

You and your friend both decide to have the same bet, you forecasting that India will score *under* 400 runs, your friend *over* 400 runs. And, instead of the flat £20, wager you now both bet £1 a run. This means that for every run India scores under 400 you will profit by £1 multiplied by that number. And, conversely, for every run that is scored over 400 you will lose £1 multiplied by the number.

You have effectively sold Indian runs short at 400.

Short selling, or the ability to make money from falling prices can be a very powerful tool in your trading arsenal. Just imagine if you had been convinced the dotcom boom would end in tears and you had acted on that view and sold Boo.com, Lastminute.com, Amazon.com . Lets face it you wouldn't be sitting reading an investment book right now!

You may feel today that it's something you don't want to get involved in, but what about in the future? It's therefore essential that you understand the mechanics of a short transaction, how you make, or lose, and the associated advantages and disadvantages of such an investment strategy.

However, it might be said that short selling is 'hardly cricket' because you are selling something you do not own! Yes, but . . . forget any qualms you may have on that score. Short selling is not only an accepted convention in financial markets, it is very widely used (and profited from) and it helps to keep the fluidity and liquidity that we all want from financial markets.

UNDERSTAND SHORT SELLING IN STAGES

Too many people get confused with short selling because they try and understand everything about it at once. Sometimes the actual mechanics and paperwork behind short selling can be complicated, but like most financial products or concepts the process of understanding it is made so much clearer if you break it down piece by piece.

Once you understand the concepts, short selling is actually very simple, but it can take time for the knowledge to sink in. You *must*, therefore, concentrate on this topic, as you will know when you understand the principles of short selling, in the same way that you know when you can or can't ride a bike! Do not proceed in the marketplace until you have that feeling.

We are great enthusiasts for short selling. However, the bad news is we cannot find a UK broker who offers the facility, US brokers – no problem but UK brokers are in the Dark Ages. The good news is you can short sell in the UK using contracts for difference and spread betting (see Chapters 5 and 8). This chapter will give you the basics for both instruments and for when UK brokers start offering a proper service.

SHORT SELLING BASICS

- Short selling is a concept of trading that allows investors to profit from a *fall* in a price of an instrument rather than a rise.
- The key to fully understanding short selling is to break it down into simple, understandable concepts.
- Traditional investing or speculation has always been about rising markets. An investor buys ABC stock at £1.00 per share and then sells it in the future at £1.25 turning in a £0.25 profit per share.
- Short selling is the opposite. Instead of a trader buying ABC shares because he is optimistic, he sells them short because he has a bearish

outlook. He therefore sells (to open a short position) the share at £1.00 to go what is effectively known as 'short'. Take the assumption that the price does decline and a profit of £0.30 is taken by 'covering' or buying the short position at £0.70.

● Do not start to get sidelined by the fact of owning or not owning the share or instrument, it will only confuse. Just concentrate on the mathematics of what is involved and how a profit or loss is made.

RETURNING TO THE CRICKET ANALOGY

There are three possible outcomes for the short trade:

1 **A winning trade**

India score 325 runs.

400 (the level at which you went short) – 325 (final score) = 75 runs.

75 runs × £1 (per run) = £75 profit.

2 **A losing trade**

India score 450 runs

400 (the level at which you went short) – 450 (final score) = –50 runs.

–50 runs × £1 (per run) = –£50 loss.

3 **Breakeven trade**

India score 400 runs.

400 (the level at which you went short) – 400 (final score) = 0 runs.

0 × £1 = no profit/loss.

We think you'll now agree that understanding the profit and loss profile of a short trade is simple. And, incidentally, you can trade cricket runs both long and short in exactly the same format as above using spread betting (see Chapter 8). So now if we translate this cricket example into the stockmarket instead of selling Indian cricket runs at 400, we sell short XYZ share at 400p.

Example

An example of short selling – Vodafone

Vodafone shares are trading at 150p–151p (bid–offer spread). You are bearish of the stock, expecting prices to decline. You therefore instruct your broker to sell

1,000 shares short at 150p to initiate a short position. You will therefore make money if the price declines and lose if the price of Vodafone rises. There are three possible results for the short seller:

1 **A winning trade – Vodafone shares drop to 125p**

   What is your profit?

   150p (initial short price) – 125p (present price) = 25p.

   1,000 (shares) × 25p (share decline) = profit of £250.

2 **A losing trade – Vodafone shares rise to 180p**

   What is your loss?

   150p (initial short price) – 180p (present price) = –30p.

   1,000 (shares) × –30p (share rise) = –£300 loss.

3 **A breakeven trade – Vodafone shares at 150p**

   150p – 150p = zero

   1,000 (shares) × 0 = £ zero

The chart shown in Figure 2.1 relates to the Vodafone example above.

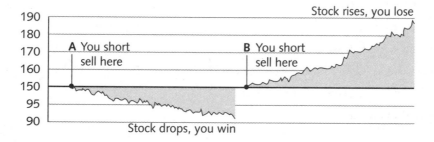

Figure 2.1 Short selling example

WHAT GOES ON BEHIND THE SCENES

As soon as most people are introduced to short selling the question 'how can you sell something you don't own?' arises. But how can you buy and sell cricket runs with your friend? You can't own the runs, you can't touch them, etc.

There are two answers to this question: the simple one and the complex. And the authors are not going to delve into the complex explanation because (a) it won't help you and (b) they are not exactly sure of the process anyway! But is this not a cop out, does it show us up to be less than knowledgeable about the inner workings of the financial markets? No, because we estimate that as many as 95 per cent of the market do not understand the back office procedures and inner workings of short selling.

Concentrate on simply understanding the mathematics of the profit and loss. When a trader is offered the ability to go short on a share, option or future, etc. the broker will take care of all the paperwork and what goes on behind the scenes. Your job by trading is to make money; the broker's job is to provide you with the tools and set-up to enable you to do this.

CAUGHT SHORT

There are dangers in short selling. The most important danger is that you expose your capital. Let us say you sold 1,000 Safeway short at 250p because you thought it was performing poorly and that its results would be dismal. But just before the results were due the US supermarket chain Wal Mart put in a bid for Safeway and the shares rocketed to 500p as Uncle Tom Cobbleigh, Tesco, Sainsbury's and all decided they could make the supermarket profitable.

You may not have yourself to blame; you may have thought through the possibility of a takeover bid but rejected it because you thought all the major UK supermarkets would have competition problems if they tried to expand their market share.

You were wrong. You are now left short covering, scrambling to find the shares to deliver and you can't buy them for a penny less than fiver. Theoretically there is no limit on how high a share can rise so, theoretically there is no limit on your ultimate exposure.

The risk of takeover is always a scare tactic used by people who discourage short selling and while it is true there is a risk there are two points a short seller has to realize. First, just how often do surprise takeovers happen and, second, what about profits warnings where share prices often drop by 25 per cent or more in a flash. There are, in our opinion, just as many potential risks to the buyer of shares as there are to the short seller.

SHORT SELLING & SHORT-TERM TRADING

Short selling is not really an investment strategy, rather a trading one. A lot of money has been made since the peak of stock prices back in the years

2000/2001 but these traders are not 'short-and-hold' types (if that phrase exists!), rather they can be viewed as hit-and-run traders, sell the stock short and look to cover it certainly within a month or so.

Short sellers also know that in bear markets the hardest and sharpest movements tend to come in the form of rising prices, so called bear market rallies. Just look at the movements of Wall Street from October 2002 onwards and you'll see that stocks and indexes can easily move up 10–20 per cent in a matter of days, even though the overall trend remains downward. The bottom line when short selling is take your profits and don't overstay your welcome.

SHORT SELLING ON UK STOCKS

For most if not all retail clients short selling is not allowed through your regular stockbroker, but while this was a problem pre-1995, with the advent of Contracts for Differences or CFDs (discussed in Chapter 5) and spread bets (Chapter 8) even clients with small accounts can take advantage of the short side of the market. Companies like E*TRADE (www.etrade.com) for CFDs and CityIndex (www.cityindex.co.uk) for spread bets offer their clients the ability to trade the short side as well as using stop losses.

→ summary

Short selling is a relatively simple concept. It is also an important part of any trader's toolbox for it means that they can not only profit from bearish moves in stocks, options or indexes but can also use some of these instruments to effectively hedge or take protection over investments that will suffer in declining markets.

One area where traders new to these concepts always seem to get bogged down is in the theory behind the process. As we have mentioned before, the question of how one can sell stock that one does not own is often asked. Leave the market mechanics to the brokers, they have extremely sophisticated back offices and processes that deal with these issues, the important question for the traders to understand is simple – How do I make and lose money by short selling?

3

Charting

MAPPING YOUR WAY THROUGH CHARTS

When you set out on a car trip you normally take a map. But a ship's captain embarking on a voyage will take charts. His journey is more difficult because the route he takes will be subject to tides, winds and currents and he will have to check his position on a regular basis to ensure he's on the right course. When you set off on a journey in the stock market your destination is always 'Profit'. There are many ways of getting there and your course is beset by many more influences than that of the ship's captain.

Love them or loath them charts can help you in taking your bearings in the financial markets and should be in every trader's toolbox, especially if you are trading short term. But one of the inherent problems with charts is the misconception that they can somehow predict prices. Thinking like this will only get you into trouble. Instead you should view charts as nothing more than simple probability tools. For example, if the price of a stock moves to a certain level, then the probabilities are in favour of that stock moving to, say, a higher level.

We see charts as something of a secret weapon in the war against risk. No, they don't prescribe what you should do next but they do reveal probabilities. The philosopher Hegel said that there is one thing man learns from history and that is that man learns nothing from history. Never fall into the trap of believing that past performance is any indicator of future outcome – but there may be some clues there. In a sense charts reduce your choices in a helpful way by focusing on what is more or less risky, what is or is not possible. There is a common sense to charts which we find appealing.

CHARTING VERSUS TECHNICAL ANALYSIS

There is a big difference between charting and technical analysis (which also uses charts extensively). Charting is simple; incorporating the look and shape of the chart with perhaps a few lines or a moving average drawn on it. But technical analysis is far more complex, often using computers to number crunch alongside technical analysis indicators such as overbought/oversold indicators. An overbought/oversold market is one where price is deemed to have got too far ahead of itself as markets seldom go up or down in a straight line.

We feel that there is a power and effectiveness in using a simple approach to charts. And the added advantage is that you don't have to spend hours poring over charts in preparation for the next trading session. What you want to try and take from a chart is simply the character of the market together with any clues for future support or resistance.

DON'T DISCOUNT CHARTS

Most market participants, especially the short-term players, use charts in their trading. Even an investor who proudly boasts that charts are worth nothing will still normally pay attention to the major highs and lows of a given stock or market. Ultimately he's still looking at the price action, in reality charts are simply a visual representation of that price action.

Are charts self-fulfilling because everybody looks at them? Who knows, maybe they are, maybe not. In the same way that in markets the players are entering and exiting at different times for different reasons, people looking at charts are looking at a snapshot that may have been taken before or after the one you are holding in your hands.

But if you feel that they are a waste of time and don't work, then consider using them in a contrary fashion. If everyone is buying because the chart shows a bullish pattern, consider selling or even going short. Using tools in opposite ways to their conceived wisdom can often be a lucrative way of approaching the markets.

CHARTING EQUIPMENT

There are three sources of charts:

- Free or paid charting sites on the Internet.
- Standalone charting programs using either real-time or end-of-day data.

- Brokers who supply their clients with online trading and charting software

Good examples of Internet sites are www.yahoo.com and www.prophet.net which both have free and paid options. The Metastock charting packing by www.equis.com is one of the best standalone software programs, and the authors use this combined with end-of-day data for London stocks from www.finexprestel.com .

CONSTRUCTION OF CHARTS – THREE TYPES

Bar charts

These are the most common style of charts, a simple vertical line depicting the open, high, low and close. The small dash on the left of the bar is always the open and the dash on the right shows the close. Whether you're looking at one-minute bars or monthly bars all bar charts are drawn in a similar fashion (see Figure 3.1).

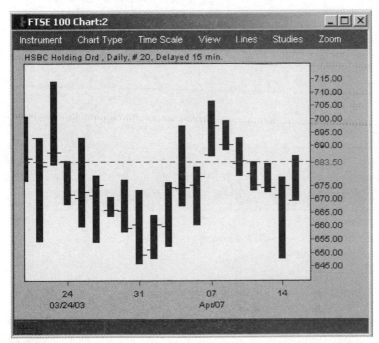

Figure 3.1 Daily bar chart – HSBC Holdings

Source: Courtesy of www.etrade.com

Line charts

These show just the closing prices of the security or market in question. Many chartists consider them inferior to bar charts because they don't show the highs or lows. Although the close is obviously important information, the highs and lows are often more so because they can sometimes be several percent away from the daily close. For example, ABC stock closes today at £5.50 but the high was £6.25. A line chart would therefore only show the £5.50 level but a bar chart would show both. Most traders disregard line charts for just this reason (see Figure 3.2).

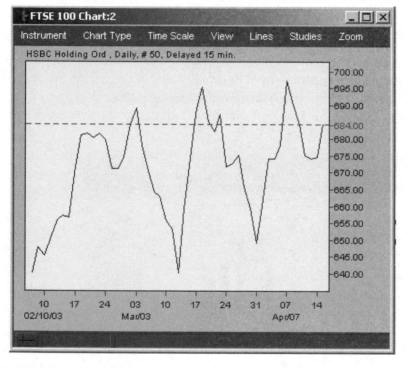

Figure 3.2 **Daily line chart – HSBC Holdings**

Source: Courtesy of www.etrade.com

Candlestick charts

Candlestick charts have become very popular over the last 10 years, and they give another perspective on the time period in question, whether intraday, daily or weekly, etc. Candlestick charts (see Figure 3.3) display the open, high, low and closing prices in a format similar to a bar chart, but

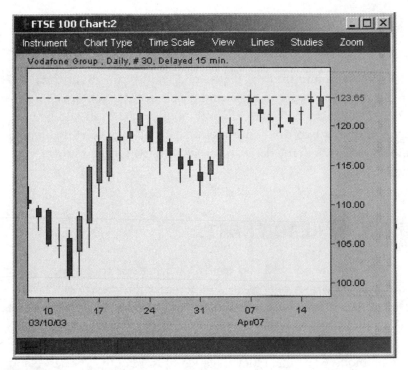

Figure 3.3 **Daily candlestick chart – Vodafone**

Source: Courtesy of www.etrade.com

show the relationships in pictorial manner. Users of candlesticks have many different phrases to describe the chart pattern that's developing, some examples are given below. For further education and advice on candlesticks there is an excellent guide at www.chartanalysts.com/introtocandles.pdf .

WHAT CHARTING METHOD SHOULD YOU USE?

Is one style of charting better than the other? Of course, with trading and analysis one may have an advantage over another in its own context. But we advise you look at either bar charts or candlesticks, and it's always good advice not to chop and change from one style to the next.

CHARTING TIMEFRAMES

The timeframe that you use for your charting should complement the time period in which you're trading. If you're a short-term trader then you should put more emphasis on the intraday charts but if you are a longer-term investor then the daily, weekly and monthly charts should be your reference. Studying two different timeframes is always worthwhile and the authors look at both the daily and weekly charts for their longer-term trading.

 ## HOW TO READ CHARTS

With charts there are no hard and fast rules, what one trader may deem bullish can be a bearish pattern to another, and this makes the task of educating difficult. It is the same with art, go to a museum with a friend and the art that appeals to you may do nothing for your friend and vice versa. Most good chartists are therefore self-taught. They approach their charts in a unique way which they have learnt from both experience and picking up ideas and tactics from other market participants.

So what should you do if you want to master charting? This is not a book on technical analysis; with one chapter we can only scratch the surface and give a little guidance. If you want to use charts in your trading first make sure you have access to a good charting source, then go and study the free charting lessons at www.investorprofit.com/charts . It is then purely a matter of practice and experience to build and use charts effectively in your trading plan.

 ## THE BASICS OF CHARTING

Flowing markets

One of the main characteristics you should look for in charts is flowing movement because movement in a market or stock means that there's money to be made. A market that is moving or trending in a certain direction often continues to do so, and you want to be looking for these trends either up or down. Flowing movement should be obvious to the eye as you can see from the examples below (Figures 3.4, 3.5, 3.6 and 3.7).

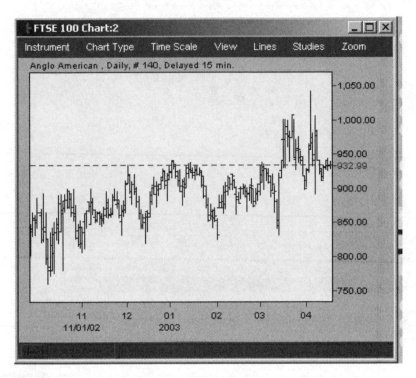

Figure 3.4 Flowing uptrend – Anglo American daily bar chart

Source: Courtesy of www.etrade.com

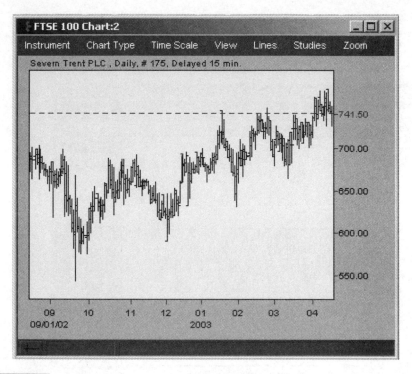

Figure 3.5 Flowing uptrend – Severn Trent daily bar chart

Source: Courtesy of www.etrade.com

Figure 3.6 Flowing downtrend – Abbey National

Source: Courtesy of www.etrade.com

Figure 3.7 **Flowing downtrend – Hays plc**

Source: Courtesy of www.etrade.com

Trading ranges

Trading ranges (Figures 3.8, 3.9 and 3.10) should be clearly visible and you should be instantly able to pick them out. Markets within trading ranges are normally problematic to trade and it is normally good advice to wait until price moves out of the range before committing funds. Or perhaps if you want to go long, one idea would be to stagger your buy orders at the lower extremes of the range.

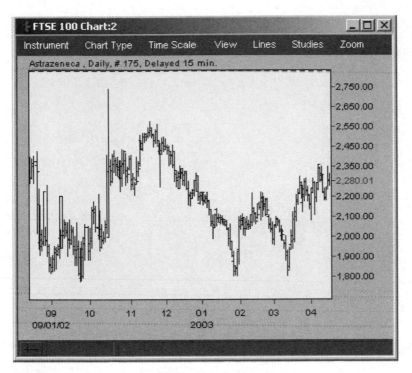

Figure 3.8 Trading range – AstraZeneca daily chart

Source: Courtesy of www.etrade.com

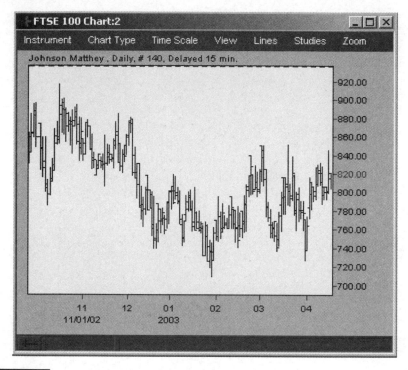

Figure 3.9   Trading range – Johnson Mathey

Source: Courtesy of www.etrade.com

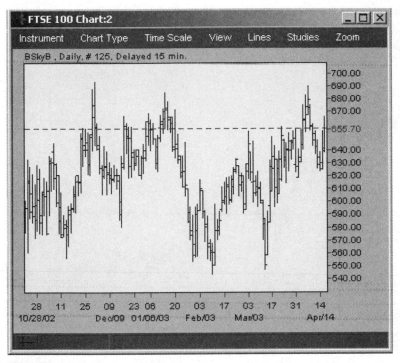

Figure 3.10 Trading range – BSkyB daily chart

Source: Courtesy of www.etrade.com

Using charts as a safeguard

A good use for charts is as a safeguard to try to keep you out of trouble or stop foolish trades. In the examples below (Figures 3.11 and 3.12) it is obvious that the major trend is down and it's certainly hard to feel bullish about the stock. Bottom fishing always gives the illusion of being profitable but it's unlikely that your timing will be right, and therefore the stock will often have further to fall. Using charts from a defensive point of view is one way to keep traders out of trouble. The concept is again simple to understand and implement, if you've got a negative looking chart think twice about committing funds.

Figure 3.11 Sainsbury's daily chart – does the price action inspire confidence?

Source: Courtesy of www.etrade.com

Figure 3.12 Reuters' daily chart – does the price action inspire confidence?

Source: Courtesy of www.etrade.com

Identify support and resistance levels

Charts are excellent tools for determining potential support and resistance levels. Identifying these levels is easier than you think. Look for the old major highs and lows on the chart that stand out. In Figure 3.13, the chart on Aviva shows where obvious buying and selling came in and the two horizontal lines, and therefore these levels, can be viewed as future support and resistance should the market go there. Some market participants wonder why these areas are significant but as we mentioned at the beginning of the chapter charting or technical analysis are nothing more than a series of probability statements about the market, therefore as the market has attracted some buying before at a certain level it is probable that this will occur again.

So how can one use support and resistance levels? We like to use them as either targets for buying or selling. For example, on the Aviva chart if we had been buying the shares at around the £3.50 level then the resistance at around £5.75 would be a target that we'd be looking to take profits at. And the reverse would be true if we were trading short, we'd look to take some or all of our profits at a level around £3.50.

Figure 3.13 Aviva daily chart

Source: Courtesy of www.etrade.com

Relative movement

Relative movement using charts is a sound way of evaluating different stocks or markets and it's very simple. Look at two stock charts from the same sector (or similar markets such as NASDAQ vs Dow Jones 30) and see how they are moving in relationship to each other. What you want to be looking for are clear signs of over- or under-performance between the two. For example, a trader may well become bullish about the telecom sector but which stock or stocks should he buy and which are better left alone? Using relative strength is often a good way to answer these kinds of question?

Look at Figures 3.14 and 3.15 and the concept of relative strength should be obvious. Here we have daily charts of the FTSE 100 and the US NASDAQ 100 and it is clear that while both markets are down the NASDAQ is obviously out-performing the FTSE. This is especially apparent when you look at the recent lows of 2002 for while the FTSE was making subsequent lower lows the NASDAQ market was nowhere near violating its 2002 lows. If you were looking to go long either in the UK or US markets then the NASDAQ would be a better candidate using the principles of relative strength because the chart and overall price context just looks and feels more supportive. This type of analysis also works well when looking for potential short candidates.

Figure 3.14 **FTSE 100 Cash – daily chart**

Source: Courtesy of www.etrade.com

Short-term and day traders often rely heavily on relative strength concepts. In Europe there are at least six major stock indexes all tending to move in the same direction. On most days it's unlikely that the German DAX will be up 2 per cent, the FTSE down 3 per cent, the Italian MIB30

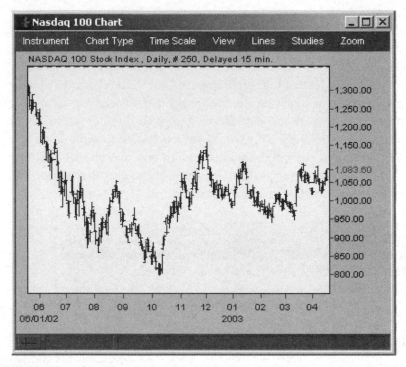

Figure 3.15 US NASDAQ 100 Cash – daily chart

Source: Courtesy of www.etrade.com

unchanged, etc. The bourses all tend to move either up or down together but the percentage movements will be different. So a short-term trader looking to go long stock indexes will often try and trade the 'better' or strongest performer. If the German DAX is making new highs for the day while the FTSE is turning in a sluggish performance, traders will often concentrate their buying in the DAX. Using relative strength is all about identifying momentum and joining it.

Chart patterns

Chartists have a language of their own. Many traders like to look for chart patterns with such names as 'head and shoulders', 'pennants', 'ascending triangles' and the like. These patterns are all subjective with their interpretation always down to the individual. As we've mentioned before there's no rulebook or set theory behind any of the concepts of charting. However, we prefer to look more at the visual character and shape of the chart believing that it is more important and robust than these standard textbook patterns.

However, like any aspect of charting analysis some traders have found these types of pattern invaluable. One interesting area for further research would be to investigate what happens to the market if these widely followed patterns fail? For example, say traders are focusing on a well known bullish chart pattern on Vodafone: most market participants will be looking to trade textbook style, all going long at around the same price, with associated stop losses in the same area. But what happens if the chart pattern fails, and the market doesn't move in the anticipated direction? In this case there's going to be an awful lot of selling while traders scramble for the exit, most probably at the same time. A few traders over the years have built their careers looking for just this kind of 'failed' reversal pattern in that they will patiently wait until the pattern looks like it's breaking down and then go aggressively long or short (depending on whether it was a bullish or bearish pattern) hoping to catch the majority of market participants on the hop.

For further details on chart pattern go to the free charting lessons on the investorprofit.com website.

Using chart analysis for context

Context is always about having a reason for a trade. A lot of money is lost or wasted by traders not having concrete reasons for the trade. Betting on a horse because you like its name or colour is not the correct way to bet at the races, and a similar approach in the markets will not generate good results.

When you initiate a position you should always have sound and logical reasons behind the trade, not wishy-washy ideas full of hope or hunches. It is part of the message throughout this book of understanding what you are doing. Using charts can be an excellent way to base your trading decisions on 'context'. This context could be how the chart looks or perhaps the failure of a commonly known chart pattern as discussed above. If you're looking to sell a stock at a certain level, why that level? Try and have some context like an old high on the chart to play against. Start to question yourself *before* you do a trade and make sure that you give yourself good, valid and sensible reasons as to why you're buying or selling. If you start this practice before you trade and you find your arguments unconvincing or weak, don't do the trade.

TECHNICAL INDICATORS

Pick up any book on technical analysis and you'll see a myriad indicators that can be used to generate buy and sell signals. Indicators such as stochastics, MACD, momentum, cycles, etc. – there are too many to list. The question remains, are they useful, will they help you make money, or lose less when you're wrong? Unfortunately the answer is ambiguous. Every technical indicator will work some of the time and be useless at others. Knowing when to use them and when not to is 90 per cent of the battle.

What you ultimately have to remember about technical indicators is that because they are based on price action all indicators are lagging in their nature, meaning that they normally react *after* an event. This is why placing more emphasis on the simple daily and weekly price action is a better way to trade than relying on technical indicators. If price is the dominant factor in trading then there are strong arguments for not diluting it by using technical indicators that will always lag.

If you do decide to investigate some of these technical indicators be very wary of falling into the trap of chopping and changing every week from one to the next, hoping each time that the next tool will put you on easy street. It's a problem from which many traders suffer. Chopping and changing will never work because you won't give yourself enough time to understand the nuances of the different methods, and this is the real key with any type of analysis technique – learn when they can be relied on and when they can't.

 FURTHER EDUCATION ON TECHNICAL ANALYSIS AND CHARTING

The Internet is a fabulous place for researching almost any topic, especially the technical nature of trading the markets. There are literally hundreds of sites for every level of understanding and you'd be well advised to take a few hours researching what's available. Be very careful about sites charging lots of money and giving the impression that they have some new system, or technical indicator that makes a lot of money. A tiny percentage of pay sites are worth it, but it will take experience and some knowledge to find them. Also, realize that a lot of information that is sold on the Internet is just a repackaging of the same material you can find elsewhere for free.

→ **summary**

Charts are an excellent addition to any investor's toolbox as long as you don't get any illusions that they can predict price. As we pointed out in the Introduction, just use them to gauge probabilities. They should also not be viewed as a quick way to get rich and traders new to the game should be exceptionally wary of anyone that tries to tell you different.

If you want to get good with charts, first realize that there is no right or wrong way to use them, no rules so to speak, and, second, study them over and over again. Look at them after the close everyday, but don't look for something specific, let something interesting find you. And while this point is hard to understand if you practice it you will soon see the benefit. The more charts you study the better the feel you'll get, and this is ultimately what you want charts to offer you – the character and feel of the market or stock in question.

Remember that, like a ship's captain's use of charts, charting is not an exact science. A ship's captain uses the charts as a guide, all the time his ship is moving it is subject to different influences and the sea and seabed are also changing continuously. In the time it takes to print out a chart you may wish to use the markets will have changed and the influences on the indicators will have altered. This is not a problem; simply a reminder for us to *use* charts not let them determine our strategy.

4

Stop losses – how to win by losing

CUT YOUR LOSSES AND LET YOUR PROFITS RUN

This adage used by market professionals is another foundation of successful trading. Ignoring it is also the main reason why most non-professional investors achieve indifferent performances. The aim of this chapter is to help you understand what stop losses are, how they work as well as when and where to place them.

WHY IS LIMITING YOUR LOSSES SO IMPORTANT?

Limiting your losses can make you money by default. Most people believe that the best traders are always the ones who buy and sell at the better prices, e.g. where you buy a stock at £5.00 and sell it at £5.50. A more profitable trader buys the same stock at £4.00 and sells it at £6.00. But the reason why some traders get better results is often a lot simpler.

There were two traders . . . .

Trader A and Trader B meet to discuss their business. Trader A reports that he made £100k for the year while Trader B reports a profit of £50k. Both want to improve their trading records by going to a 'trading coach'. The coach tells them to make two separate piles of the past year's trading statements, all their winning trades (whether £1 or £1,000) in one pile, and all their losing trades in the other.

What the coach sees is this:

	Trader A	Trader B
Winners	£150k	£150k
Losers	£50k	£100k
Net result	£100k profit	£50k profit

The coach tells Trader A that he is very effective at making money and very 'effective' at not losing too much. The coach wishes him luck for the following year.

But, the coach has a very important observation for Trader B. He shows B that he is *just* as effective at making money at his pal A: he is as good as A at picking good trades and making good profits. But where Trader B falls down is on losses. The coach tells B that he is nowhere near as effective at handling or managing his losses as A. What is more, if he can reduce his losses just 25 per cent then his overall winnings would rocket by 50 per cent.

You can see from this that making more money is not just about picking more winners. What you need to do is pick fewer losers!

Intelligent use of stop loss orders is one of the main ways that you can 'lose less' and make money by default. Look at your trading record for last year and see how you could have improved your profits by cutting your losses.

WHAT IS A STOP LOSS?

A stop loss is what it says: an order to stop your losses. In taking a loss you are preventing any further loss. From now on in this book we will normally refer to stop losses simply as 'stops'.

Stops were originally introduced in the fast moving futures markets. Because of the leverage on offer both big profits and losses can be accrued in a short period of time. Leverage in the markets normally means you can control 100 per cent of the value of the asset for around a 5–20 per cent deposit or 'margin'. If you buy £10k of BT stock, the maximum that you can lose on your original capital is £10k if BT were to go bust. But if you buy £10k worth of BT stock on margin (for example, putting up 10 per cent or £1,000) then even a small sell-off in BT can quickly wipe out your capital.

Stops are second nature to futures brokers: placing a stop order is as common as a buy or sell order. Every broker not only knows what they are and how to place them, they are also set up to handle them. But this is not the case in the stock market where active use of stop losses in the UK market only began around 1996.

From the futures market to the stock market

Pre-1996 the stock market was viewed by futures traders as altogether too slow and boring because it lacked the volatility on which they thrived. Large movements, both up and down, of course, occurred, but not with the speed and regularity that the futures market offered. But 1995 and the start of the great stockmarket bubble changed all of this. Here was a market that suddenly offered incredible movement on a daily and weekly basis and futures traders decided that this was something they wanted to be part of.

This is how stop losses migrated to the stock market. However, the transition wasn't seamless. Stockbrokers were generally unfamiliar with stops and even today most of them don't understand how to apply them. Many UK stockbrokers simply won't take them as orders thus denying their clients one of the most valuable tools in the investor's toolkit. The US stockmarket, though, is more mature with most if not all stockbrokers willing normally via their software packages to offer clients the ability to execute stop losses.

A stop loss is generally a day order only – they have to be renewed every day. If you had a good relationship with your broker he might accept a stop loss order to stop out at a given level when you are away on holiday for example. But the normal practice is that stop loss orders lapse at the end of each day.

We are assuming that most of the readers will use stops as a safeguard against purchases (long positions) that they make in the stock market, as opposed to short positions. For this reason we will only be dealing with 'sell stop loss' orders as opposed to 'buy stop' orders. For readers that are interested in using stops for short positions they work in exactly the same way except in reverse, a buy order being substituted for a sell order.

HOW STOP LOSS ORDERS WORK

Imagine calling your broker up and instructing him to sell 1,000 shares of Vodafone 'at the market'. The broker will simply pull up the Vodafone dealing screen, enter 1,000 shares and click 'sell'. The computer will then automatically sell those shares at the current bid price. That is a 'market sell order'.

A stop loss order shares many of the same characteristics of a simple 'market order' but is 'held back' from actually being activated until the stock price trades at the stop loss level. Therefore if the price of Vodafone is £1.00 and you wanted to sell 1,000 Vodafone at £0.90 on a sell stop, this order will not be activated *unless* Vodafone traded down to £0.90 or below. The moment Vodafone starts trading at £0.90 the sell stop immediately becomes a 'market sell order' and the 1,000 shares are sold on the bid. But be careful – you might not actually sell at £0.90 a share.

The reason you might not sell at £0.90 is that market orders are always traded at the best possible market price – not necessarily the price that you want to trade at. Let us look at a simple market sell order for the time being and forget about stop losses. You call your broker asking for a quote on Vodafone, he reports 100–100.5. You then instruct him to sell 1,000 shares 'at market', but when he places the order the bid–offer has suddenly dropped to 99.5–100. You would therefore be selling at 99.5, not 100.

This is why stop losses are often not executed at the price of the original order, because they are a hybrid market order. The original sell stop order to sell 1,000 Vodafone at £0.90 becomes a market order to sell 1,000 Vodafone as soon as the share price trades at £0.90. But in a quick or volatile market by the time the order is actually transacted (perhaps less than 20 seconds), the price has fallen through £0.90 and the order is actually filled at say £0.89.

This should not deter you from using stops. Selling out at less than the sell order whether it is a market order or a stop is part of the market process. Our view is that it is definitely better to have stops than not have them but take the slippage (described on page 76) on the chin.

 ## STOP LOSSES ARE PERVERSE

Stop loss orders will frustrate you. If you are using them to dump a losing position then their application will always mean bad news. You will not only have been proved wrong in your market judgement, you will also have lost money. The most frustrating aspect of stop losses is when you sell your losing position on the low of the day before the market suddenly turns around and moves dramatically higher.

Situations like this happen to all traders who use stops, and what you must realize is that using a stop loss on any individual trade, with hindsight, may not have been the correct thing to do. But using a stop loss policy on a *series of trades* is the critical point. If you do this then there will be times when they infuriate you but also times when they preserve serious amounts of your capital. Try to get into the habit of thinking that a single trade is never that important, it is the *series of trades* over a period of time that is significant.

EXPERIENCE IS IMPORTANT WHEN PLACING STOPS

There is no exact science when deciding at what level to place a stop loss. Sometimes many factors come into play and experience is often the key when deciding the right level at which to place them. Perversely you will find that you learn a fair amount from putting your stops in the wrong place! While this is bad news in the short term, it is often good news over the long run. Learning from your mistakes is the best education a trader or investor can receive. But, of course, 'stops' can help to make that learning experience less painful.

The main error people make when first using stops is to place them far too near to where the market is trading. If you want to cut down on the number of errors that you make when you start out, then try to place your stops far away from the current market price, giving the market plenty of room to move around without stopping you out.

KEEP FLEXIBLE WITH STOPS BUT . . .

It is important always to have a stop loss in place and it is common practice among traders to move this level as the market or your opinion changes. But it is wise *never* to move the sell stop to a lower level. If you buy 1,000 shares in Abbey National at £6.00 with a £5.30 sell stop, do not move this lower. This is a common error that traders make. They place a stop loss order in a sensible area only for them to cancel it and move it to a lower level if the market starts threatening it. They will often do this a few times, usually leading to far greater losses.

DIFFERENT TYPES OF STOP LOSS ORDERS

Technical Stops

Technical stops are how professionals usually operate and are highly recommended. The word 'technical' simply refers to the fact that the stop levels are based on charts. These stops make sense because they force you to place them above or below price levels of trading that have some sort of relevance. An example of a technical stop is below a daily or weekly low, or a price level where the market has found some previous support or buying interest. The advantage of using these kinds of stops is that your trading will start to be dictated by what the market is doing, rather than your gut feel and guesswork.

Try and find lows that stand out to place stop losses behind. In Figure 4.1, once Anglo American started rallying in May, the April low was very pronounced. Seek to place your stops below such levels. But with the low at £10.20, what should the actual price level of your stop be?

Perversity in the markets will hound traders most of the time. If you place the stop loss at £10.15 the market will often move to £10.10 before moving back up. If you place the stop loss at £9.90 the market will often go through it. What we advise is simple: look at the recent market character

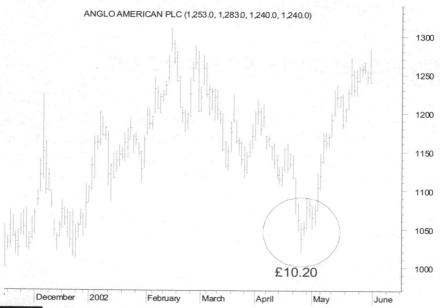

ANGLO AMERICAN PLC (1,253.0, 1,283.0, 1,240.0, 1,240.0)

£10.20

December 2002 February March April May June

Figure 4.1 **Example of technical stops – recent lows**

and then make an assumption on how volatile it is. If it is volatile then use a wider stop and vice versa. In this case we would say that the market is not particularly volatile and so a stop at around £10.10 would make sense.

In the example shown in Figure 4.2, we have another standout low (once the market starts rallying at the end of May). Again using common sense we take the view that there is not much volatility in the share so our stop would be around £5.77.

In the example shown in Figure 4.3, if we're going to purchase shares in BSkyB (some time in July) then the most relevant low for our stop to work against would be the September 2001 level of £5.16. (Incidentally don't be worried about using levels that are in some cases many months or even years old, this does not matter at all.) Here we see a volatile market and we would prefer to use a much wider stop loss level well below the September low, somewhere around £4.75–£4.80. Because the market is volatile we're trying to give it the maximum amount of room to move about before stopping us out. It would be unfortunate if the stop were placed at £5.10 only for the market to sell off down to £5.00 before rallying sharply without us on board.

Think carefully, use some common sense, and always try to give the market a fair amount of room to move before you're actually stopped out.

Figure 4.2   Example of technical stops – recent lows

B SKY B (581.5, 600.0, 579.5, 595.5)

£5.16

Apr | May | Jun | Jul | Aug | Sep | Oct | Nov | Dec | 2002 | Feb | Mar | Apr | May | Jun | Jul

Figure 4.3 Example of technical stops – recent lows

Monetary stops

The simplest stop losses are monetary or percentage stops, they give you instant knowledge of what your loss will be. You buy 5,000 shares of XYZ at £1.37 and decide to risk £1,000 (commissions and stamp duty excluded). A simple calculation means that you would place your stop loss at £1.17.

The disadvantage of monetary stops is that they are placed at arbitrary levels and they mean nothing as far as the market goes. It is far better to place your stops below or above meaningful levels such as a recent low or below some support that you can see on the chart, as with 'technical stops' discussed above.

Percentage stops

You buy a share at £5.00 and decide to place your stop loss, say, 20 per cent away from the purchase price, meaning a level of £4.00. Again these types of stops are easy and simple. If you use percentage stops then you have to try and gauge the character of the market you're trading in. Setting a 5 per cent stop loss on Tesco is not the same as a 5 per cent stop on Vodafone because Vodafone is far more volatile than Tesco. So perhaps a 5 per cent stop on Tesco would perhaps translate to a 15 per cent stop on Vodafone.

The disadvantage of 'percentage stops' is similar to 'monetary stops', they are always placed at an arbitrary level. But remember the critical point with stop losses: having one is far more important than the actual level or method you use for deciding their levels.

Using the most recent high or low for short-term trading

Stop losses placed above a recent high (buy stops) or below a recent low (sell stops) are often used in shorter-term trading. The previous day's high/low is a favourite place for day traders to place their stops behind.

But for short-term traders how many points above/below a recent high or low should the stop loss level be? Good traders tend to remain flexible and move with the underlying market fashion. For example, say the FTSE 100 future has a recent low of 4,255 and the market is and has been very volatile. It would not be wise to place the stop a few points below it, somewhere between 10–30 points would be better. Obviously, if the market has been quiet then around 5–10 ticks below the 4,255 level would be more acceptable.

Longer-term traders can also use recent highs and lows for guidance in stop placement. But instead of using the previous daily low, why not use the previous week or month's low. This is normally a far better place to put your stop than a fixed percentage or monetary amount because again you're letting the market guide you as to where to place stops.

Opening gap rule

This stop loss strategy is heavily used by some short-term traders. A trader at the beginning of the week buys 5,000 Vodafone at £1.00 looking for a quick move higher. He places his stop loss at £0.95. The stop lapses at the end of the day and overnight something disastrous is announced and the shares open the following day at £0.89. What should he do? Sell the shares immediately on the opening or freeze? Not knowing what to do is not an option, and selling on the opening is normally a bad trade because of the blind panic.

The best advice is to wait anywhere from 10–30 minutes and then place your stop a point below the low of the opening range. If the stock opens at

£0.89 and £0.88 is the low in the first 20 minutes, place your stop at £0.87. You will often find that in situations like this £0.88 will be the low for the day. We would still advise that you sell out at the original stop level should the market move back up to £0.95.

Time stops – three period rule

Many investors relate to the fact that successful trades often work from their onset. You buy a share, it moves higher and then continues to build profits. Losing trades also have a habit of doing this but in reverse. Almost straight away they go down or just meander, showing immediate losses.

The 'three period rule' is designed to force you out of trades that are simply not performing as you had expected. You might buy 2,000 Boots at £6.00 at the beginning of October, only for the price to be still wallowing around £6.00 a month or so later. Clearly you did not expect this to happen otherwise why not stay in cash and then buy a month later? It is highly probable that you are unlikely to show much profit from these positions. Our experience is that if a trade does show a profit quickly then it is better to go back into cash and re-evaluate the situation.

The three period rule was initially designed by day traders but it has been successfully carried over into long-term investing. A day trader will often use something like a 60-minute bar chart to trade off, with 60 minutes being one period. So three periods as in the 'three period rule' will amount to three hours of trading. Therefore if the trader buys a position at 9am and it's not in profit by 12pm (or shows only a tiny profit), he will look for a way out by either selling it immediately or tightening up the original stop.

Long-term investors often like to use a weekly chart, therefore the three period rule would be three weeks. If you bought Whitbread at the beginning of the month and three weeks later the stock is down or has done nothing then seriously consider selling out or moving your stop loss to a tighter level nearer the current price.

Trailing stops

A trailing stop is where you move the stop level higher as the underlying stock moves higher. If you were using a 20 per cent trailing stop loss and you buy a share at £1.00, the stop loss is £0.80. The share price then moves up to £1.20, and so you move the stop loss up to £0.96. The stock then falls back down to £1.10 before moving up to £1.50, the 20 per cent trailing stop is now moved to £1.20, etc.

If you determine the level of your stop from charts then you can still use a trailing stop loss. As the stock moves higher raise your stop to under significant levels on the chart or below the previous week's low, etc.

Breakeven stops

A breakeven stop is a stop loss order that is placed at the same level as you bought the shares. Obviously though the shares will have to move higher before utilizing a breakeven stop.

For example, you buy 1,000 shares in BT at £2.50 and the shares rise to £3.00. It's now a good time to place a breakeven stop at £2.50. In the volatile markets that we have been experiencing over the last few years' profits can both be made and lost quickly, so using a stop such as this is a good way of protecting your account.

However, you have to strike some sort of balance as to how far the share moves before you can place a breakeven stop. If you buy BT at £2.50 then clearly moving your original stop up to breakeven if the share price rises just 5p to £2.55 is ridiculous.

TIGHT VERSUS WIDE STOPS

A trader buys 1,000 shares at £2.00 and either looks to place his stop at £1.90 (stop loss A) or at £1.50 (stop loss B).

Which stop loss (A or B) carries more risk? Most people will instantly say stop B because it risks £0.50 versus £0.10 for stop A. Looking at it on a purely monetary basis this is correct but you must also look at it on a probability basis as well.

With a tight stop the share could easily move down £0.10 but not so easily by £0.50. Hence there is a trade-off between having a tight stop with a high probability of being stopped out, and having a wide stop with a reduced probability of the market moving to that level.

The true risk of a stop loss is therefore the number of points of risk alongside the probability of that level being hit. This is why wide stops generally assume *less* risk on a trade than tight stops because a wider stop is less likely to be hit during everyday market moves. Clearly though some balance has to be struck.

This is critical information because many investors when they first start using stops generally place them too near the current price thinking that they'll lose less money when wrong. On any given trade they are correct but over a series of trades placing your stop loss further away from the present price is normally the better option. If in doubt always use a wider stop loss especially in volatile shares or markets.

CAN LOSING MONEY BE A GOOD TRADE?

Getting stopped out on the low of the day never makes one feel good. But you will often find that with hindsight it can turn out to be a nice trade because the market may well move much lower over the coming days or weeks.

Many people also think that their best trades are the ones which make the most money and although that is often the case, trades that you get stopped out can sometimes turn out to be excellent as well. Imagine you had bought Marconi at £10.00 and sold it using a stop loss at £7.00. Would this trade not be a candidate for 'trade of the year'?

SLIPPAGE – POSITIVE AND NEGATIVE

When setting stop levels it is also wise to take into account 'slippage.' Slippage goes hand and hand with stop losses and there is very little that you can do to prevent it. Slippage is simply the difference between where your stop loss level is and where you actually get filled or sell the shares.

For example, you have bought 5,000 shares in BP at £6.00 and want to protect your losses should the share price move lower. You therefore decide to place a stop order to sell 5,000 BP at £5.25.

The market suddenly plunges lower and as soon as the share price trades at £5.25 the stop loss order becomes a 'market order' to sell 5,000 shares. However, prices may be moving quickly and because the stop order is really a market order the best available bid may well be at £5.22. If the shares are sold at that point you will have picked up £0.03 in negative slippage.

Expect negative slippage 75 per cent of the time

You will tend to find that 75 per cent of the time you will get negative slippage but don't view this as anything else but the cost of doing business. It happens to both small and large traders alike, and there is nothing you can normally do about it. For this reason it's always a good idea to factor in a little bit of negative slippage into your calculation – that way you will never be disappointed.

Slippage and liquid and illiquid stocks

Stop losses were designed for use in markets that have volume and are regularly traded. Always bear in mind that you will tend to suffer more negative slippage on illiquid stocks than liquid ones. FTSE 100 stocks will seldom give you problems but if you venture outside the FTSE 350 then just be aware that slippage will be more of a factor.

If you trade in penny stocks or other stocks of low volume then you should consider using some other form of taking acceptable losses. Stop loss orders on such stocks should be avoided because the lack of liquidity and the inherently large bid–offer spreads.

STOCKBROKER PROBLEMS WITH STOP LOSS

Most UK stockbrokers don't take stop loss orders on behalf of their clients, unless, of course, the client is very good for business. If you had a million-pound account and traded frequently then it would be very possible to get your broker to work your stop loss orders. You would just demand it and if he said no, it wouldn't take long to find a broker who suited your needs.

The three main reasons for brokers not taking stop loss orders are:

1 Stockbrokers often don't really understand them.

2 Their competitors don't offer them.

3 There are too many stocks to follow.

The first two are obvious but the third one needs some explanation. Remember that stop loss orders came from the futures markets when these markets were trading on open-outcry exchanges rather than on the computer. There were perhaps no more than 25 futures markets worldwide and each market was traded in a separate trading pit. In each pit a broker handled only the orders for that market. So on LIFFE a company had a different broker in the FTSE pit, and one in the Gilt pit, etc. The pit broker therefore only had to handle one market and one price so it was easy for him to keep tabs on all his orders.

But in the stock market there are many different stocks, all traded in one place. You can therefore see that it is very hard for a stockbroker to watch so many stocks at the same time, especially in busy and volatile periods.

If a broker took 50 different sell stop orders on 50 different stocks and 'missed' an order (didn't see the market fall through a sell stop level), he would still have an obligation to fill the client's order and make up any monetary difference through his error account. It is very hard for the broker to do business this way.

Stop loss orders are a vital tool for investors and brokers need to move with the times. The good news is that the technology is quickly becoming available for the brokers to build them into their software platforms, and forward thinking companies like E*TRADE (www.etrade.com) now offer their clients the ability to place and work stop loss orders via their online software.

THREE WAYS TO ACTIVATE STOP LOSSES WITHOUT A BROKER

As discussed, most UK stockbrokers do not take stop losses on behalf of their clients, but that should not hinder your ability to utilize them. But how can one use stops without following the market in real-time? Perhaps you have another job that's unrelated to the financial markets and can't or don't want to follow prices during the majority of the day.

There are two ways to get around this problem and both are very satisfactory. So if your broker won't accept stops then you have to have systems in place to activate them yourself.

Intraday execution

Intraday is how stops are handled in the futures markets. If at anytime during the day the market trades through a stop loss price then it's activated. Having stop loss orders worked on an intraday basis is most probably the best strategy to use.

However, as with anything in trading there are normally two sides to the coin. The advantage of having a stop loss order worked intraday is that if the market moves through your stop level and keeps moving lower then you will have sold at a better price than if you had waited to sell later, say on the close. The disadvantage is that markets often make big and wild moves during the day only for them to close well away from their intraday price extremes where your stop may well have been activated.

Market-on-close execution

Assume that Vodafone is priced at £1.00 but your broker will not take the order to sell your shares at £0.95 on a stop order. If you don't have time or are unwilling to follow the market during the day then call your broker (or check prices on the web) 10 minutes before the close and check the price of Vodafone. If it's below £0.95 then instruct him to sell the shares on the close.

But what happens if the shares are right at £0.95 with a few minutes to go? One idea may well be to sell half your position on the close and then evaluate the situation the following day.

The next day stop loss

For traders who can't follow the market either on an intraday basis or on the close there is a final option. You can activate your stop loss order at the opening the day after the share price closes below the stop loss level.

Assume that Vodafone is priced at £1.00 and your stop loss level is at £0.95. If and when the share price closes below £0.95 you would sell the shares on the opening the *following* day. However, selling the shares right on the opening may not be the wisest trade because the market often takes time to get going and offering tight bid–offer spreads. But it depends on the stock concerned; for Vodafone or other large FTSE companies it's no problem at all, good volume comes in right from the opening bell. But for smaller stocks it is often best to wait around 10–30 minutes till volume and tighter bid–offer spreads start to materialize.

Which stop strategy is the best?

They all have their associated advantages and disadvantages and we have seen different traders use all of the three styles with success. It really depends on whether you can follow the market or not. Two things are critical though, it doesn't really matter which one you use as long as you use one strategy and stick to it, don't chop and change. For example, today you trigger the stop loss orders intraday, next time on close, the third time the following morning, etc. This is not a good way to approach the problem because you will be using too many different strategies and the whole point of having stop losses in place is one of *discipline and simplicity*.

THE HIDDEN VALUE OF STOP LOSSES

Stop losses not only protect your trades, they have other benefits in helping you optimize your risk/reward appetite. On the one hand they take some of the burden off your shoulders, but on the other, they make you look at the whole investment picture and that leads to better investment decisions.

To be successful in trading you have to understand the risk/reward ratio and make your business decisions with it always in mind. Investing without looking at the potential risk is a very dangerous game, and traders who don't do this type of analysis often end up trading the wrong-sized position, whether too large or too small.

The solution to trading the right amount of stock is both simple and elegant and without some sort of risk analysis is impossible to find. This is the hidden value of stop losses.

HOW TO SET UP A TRADE CORRECTLY

Why do some investors always buy the same amount of stock? Today they buy £5,000 of Vodafone, tomorrow £5,000 of Tesco. The risk/reward profile on those two stocks is markedly different. Or perhaps they never know how much to buy. But if you know where your stop loss is, you can easily determine exactly how much stock to trade.

The first thing to do is determine how much of your trading capital you are willing to risk on each position that you purchase. Professional traders tend to risk anything between 1–5 per cent of their trading funds, or £1k–£5k on a £100k account. Here is an example.

Example

Bullish on ABC stock with a £4.00 stop loss

- Forecast ABC to rise over the next 2–3 weeks. Stock priced at £5.00.
- Stop loss of **£4.00**.
- Assign a risk level of £500 which is 2 per cent of a £25,000 trading account.
- £500/£1.00 = 500 shares to buy.
- ABC moves higher as expected and a £1.00 profit is taken.
- £1.00 × 500 shares = £500.
- If the trade had not worked then the loss would have been around £500 plus slippage and commissions.

Same example – different stop loss level

- Forecast ABC to rise. Stock is priced at £5.00.
- Assign a risk level of £500 for the trade which is 2 per cent of a £25,000 account.
- Stop loss is placed at **£4.50**.
- £500/0.50 = 1,000 shares to buy.
- ABC moves higher as expected and a £1.00 profit is taken.
- £1.00 × 1,000 shares = £1,000.
- If the trade had not worked the loss would have been around £500 plus slippage and commissions.

It is very important to realize what is going on in these examples. In *both* trades the risk of around £500 has been kept constant. But the profit potential has varied due to the different size allocation of the trade. This has only been possible due to the fact that we were able to define the risk via a stop loss before the trade was taken.

Professional traders are the masters of this kind of allocation and it is the main reason why the size of their trading positions varies tremendously. You will also find that in times of high market volatility your positions get naturally smaller (because they are using wider stops) and vice versa when the market goes quiet. This is clearly good news because sound trading should always adapt to what the market is doing.

Figure 4.4 shows an example of how a trade was set up in Bovis.

- Assume that the account was £100,000 and the risk on the trade was 1 per cent.

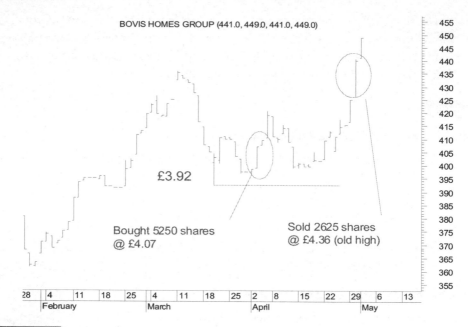

BOVIS HOMES GROUP (441.0, 449.0, 441.0, 449.0)

£3.92

Bought 5250 shares
@ £4.07

Sold 2625 shares
@ £4.36 (old high)

Figure 4.4 **Example of a trade in Bovis**

- The buying price was at £4.07.
- The most recent significant low was at £3.92.
- The sell stop was placed at £3.88, total risk was therefore £0.19 per share.
- £100,000 account, 1 per cent = £1,000.
- £1,000/£0.19 = 5,263 shares or 5,250 rounded down.
- The market moved higher and 50 per cent of the position was sold at the old high.
- What is interesting to note is that the total value of the trade was over £21,000 or 21 per cent of the account, but total risk on the account was just 1 per cent.

Incidentally the reason for selling 50 per cent of the position at the old highs was nothing more than an exercise in banking some profits while reducing risk. In situations such as this traders will often move their stop levels up to an unchanged level (same price as where they bought), so creating a trade with almost no potential loss, only further profits.

➜ **summary**

The goal of the stop loss is to define a predetermined sell level in advance using logic and reason, well before emotions regarding current news or market events cloud the decision. A good stop loss provides a perfect vehicle to cut losses fast, harvest profits when appropriate, and let winning trades run as long as possible. While other investors are pulling their hair out wondering what to do, stop losses allow the luxury of not worrying. If they are hit, sell. If not, stay in.

One of the key aspects of stops is that it's more important to have one rather than where the exact level is. If you don't know where to place a stop just use a very basic percentage stop or a monetary one. And again, don't make your stop loss policy complicated, keep it simple and logical.

Finally, you should approach every trade from the angle of risk and not reward. The first question you should be asking yourself is 'how much am I prepared to lose' should this trade move against you. Then and only then will you be approaching trading and investing the same way as the professionals.

5

Contracts For Difference

CINDERELLA CFDs

Contracts for Difference, or CFDs, allow you to trade shares utilizing margin. With a down payment of 20 per cent you control the shares with money borrowed from your broker (no, it is not an act of philanthropy on the part of your broker, he charges you interest on the extent of your borrowings).

So why not simply trade the 'real thing' and own the underlying shares? Even though you are in virtually the same position as someone who bought the shares outright there are three, very good reasons to trade CFDs:

1 You don't have to stump up all the money when you trade them.
2 CFDs are free of UK stamp duty.
3 You have the ability easily to go short shares with CFDs which you cannot with traditional shares.

To give you an example: if you purchase £10,000 of shares through your regular stockbroker you have to pay the full nominal amount. But trade £10,000 of the same stock utilizing CFDs and a deposit of only 10 to 20 per cent is required with the broker lending you the balance. This, coupled with no stamp duty (for UK shares), and the ability easily to go short shares can make them a very worthwhile addition to your financial toolbox.

So why 'Contracts for Difference?' Because they are a contract to deliver a sum of money representing the difference in price for shares on the date the contract is agreed, and the price on the day it is closed out. Ignoring the deposit, the difference is the profit or loss on the contract which, in the case of profit your broker passes on to you and in the case of a loss you have to make good to your broker.

We think that CFDs are one of the Cinderella's of the investor's toolbox. They lend great flexibility to the trader's operations but – and it is quite a substantial *but* – the cost of doing business with CFDs is high compared with other leveraged tools. We give some examples later in the chapter.

You can trade CFDs through your existing broker but it may be worth your while finding a broker who will charge a flat commission.

Examples

A simple example – long CFD

- British Telecom is trading at £1.99–£2.00
- Buy 2,000 BT using a CFD contract at £2.00.
- Nominal value of share purchase = £4,000.
- CFD deposit at 10 per cent = £400 payable by the client to the broker.
- The broker will then lend the balance of £3,600 to the client. The client will pay say 2 per cent *over* The London Inter-Bank Offer Rate (LIBOR) on the nominal amount, or £4,000, payable on a daily basis including weekends.
- LIBOR is the rate of interest at which banks normally do business with each other.

Five days later BT shares are trading at £2.10–£2.11

- Sell 4,000 BT at £2.10.
- Gross profit on deal is £0.10 × 2,000 shares = £200.
- Financing costs are £0.77* a day × 4 days = £3.08.
- Net profit on the deal is therefore £196.92 minus dealing charges, but no stamp duty at 0.5 per cent.
- The initial deposit of 10 per cent of £400 will be returned to the client's account.

* LIBOR at 5 per cent.

The profit and loss profile will be exactly the same as trading a similar amount of BT shares in the cash market. However, the return on capital will be inherently larger with CFDs because only 10 per cent of the nominal value needs to be deposited versus 100 per cent with a traditional stockbroker.

A simple example – short trade

- Barclays is trading at £5.00–£5.02.
- Sell short 1,000 shares at £5.00 using a CFD contract.
- Nominal value of share transaction = £5,000.
- CFD deposit at 10 per cent = £500 payable by the client to the broker.
- The client is now lending money to the market and will be paid (see Funding a short CFD position, page 90) say 2 per cent *under* LIBOR on the nominal amount, payable on a daily basis including weekends.

Ten days later Barclays shares are at £4.49–£4.50.

- Buy to cover 5,000 Barclays at £4.50.
- Gross profit on deal is £0.50 × 1,000 shares = £500.
- Financing costs will be a credit of around £0.41* a day × 10 days = £4.10.
- Net profit on deal is therefore £504.10 minus dealing charges, but no stamp duty of 0.5 per cent.

- The initial deposit of 10 per cent of £500 will be returned to the client's account balance.

Another example of a short trade using CFDs

- GUS is trading at £4.75–£4.77.
- Sell short 1,000 shares at £4.75.
- Nominal value of share transaction = £4,750.
- CFD deposit at 10 per cent = £475 payable by the client to the broker.
- You will now be lending money to the market and you will be paid say 2 per cent *under* LIBOR on the nominal amount, or £4,750, payable on a daily basis including weekends.

Fifteen days later the GUS price has *risen* to £5.02–£5.05.

- Buy to cover 5,000 shares at £5.05.
- Net loss on deal is £0.30 × 1,000 shares = £300.
- Financing costs will be a credit of around £0.39 a day × 15 days = £5.85.
- Gross loss on deal is therefore £294.15 plus dealing charges, but no stamp duty of 0.5 per cent.
- The initial deposit of 10 per cent or £475 is returned as cash to the client's account.

* LIBOR at 5 per cent.

HOW CAN YOU SELL SHORT STOCKS THAT YOU DON'T OWN?

The simple answer to this question is because the broker lets you. If a brokerage company has the necessary systems in place enabling you to short stocks or CFDs, then take it at face value and use the facility. While we fully understand the principles of short selling, the actual process and mechanics behind it is often complicated and we discussed our lack of knowledge of this in Chapter 2, dedicated to short selling. But the point is worth mentioning again, if you spend time trying to understand the back-office procedures behind the short sale process, will it help you become a better trader, will it enable you to make more money, or lose less when you're wrong? Of course not, so it's always better to concentrate your analysis on the market and where it's going.

FUNDING A LONG CFD POSITION

The funding of a CFD is pretty simple. On a long CFD you will be required to put up an initial margin, normally between 10 and 20 per cent. Your broker will therefore lend you the balance at a charge of around 2 per cent over LIBOR (see glossary). Although you are theoretically only being loaned 80 per cent of the CFD value you will normally pay interest on the full nominal value of the position.

If you were to purchase £10,000 worth of Vodafone stock using a CFD then the initial margin would be £1,000 with the broker lending you £9,000. If LIBOR was at 5 per cent (i.e. 5 per cent LIBOR + 2 per cent) then you would be paying an annualized rate of 7 per cent on the £10,000 that you have borrowed. This would work out at around £1.92 per day and it is payable 365 days a year – weekends and public holidays included.

If you held the long position in Vodafone for 10 calendar days, your interest bill would be about £19.00. And while borrowing money and paying interest, etc. seems very complicated, the brokers have all the necessary software to make sure the process runs very smoothly. Your statement will run a list of all debits and credits on a daily basis including those relating to interest. Of course, if you were to day trade a stock and have no position overnight, then interest is not applicable.

 ## FUNDING A SHORT CFD POSITION

The funding of a short CFD position is different from that of a long position. When you go short a stock you are *credited* interest on a daily basis, assuming of course that you hold the short position overnight. These interest payments are also credited 365 days a year. Short positions receive interest at around 2 per cent under LIBOR. As an example, with LIBOR at 5 per cent, a short position of £10,000 of stock will receive interest payable at 3 per cent, or around £0.82 per day.

It is an interesting question to note how and why a short seller receives interest. The quick but slightly ambiguous answer is because the short seller is short of stock while long on cash. But in reality unless you want to get into the details of the inner workings of CFDs it is not necessary to fully understand the exact process behind these deals. How will knowing these facts actually help you in the cut and thrust of real-time trading? Your profits and losses will come from your placing trades in the market, so concentrate your efforts there. Do as we do, if when you're short stock your broker wants to credit you money, take it!

VARIATION MARGIN

All leveraged products work with two types of margin, 'initial' and 'variation'. With CFDs the initial margin is normally the 10 to 20 per cent deposit of the nominal value of the trade. However, for some shares, notably those that are not so volatile, this deposit can be as low as 5 per cent.

All CFD positions whether long or short will be credited/debited *variation margin* on a daily basis. Assume that you buy 1,000 shares priced at £1.00, and that day the shares close at £1.05, £50 will be credited to your account in positive variation margin. Your position (although it was purchased at £1.00) will now be 'marked to market' the following day at £1.05 and not £1.00. This means that your brokerage statement now makes the assumption that you are long the shares from £1.05, not the original purchase price of £1.00 because you have already been paid the open profit.

On the second day the shares rise to £1.10 and your account will be credited another £50 in variation margin. On the third day the shares close back down at £1.00, and your account will be debited £100 in variation margin. Of course, the net monetary result from all of this movement is neither a profit nor loss until you close the contract.

Because of variation margin you must normally have an amount of free cash available in your trading account, but most CFD brokers will let you use a portion of the initial margin as payment for this but this will all depend on what positions you have, how volatile the overall stockmarket is and, of course, your relationship with the broker. As a guide, assume that you'll be able to use 25 per cent of your initial margin for variation margin purposes.

BENEFITS OF CFDS

The Ability to sell short

Before the introduction of CFDs the average UK client could not sell short on the stockmarket unless he had an excellent arrangement with his stockbroker. But with CFDs, selling short is simple: as easy as buying a share through your regular stockbroker. How do you initiate a short position? Simply sell the bid price or work an offer, exactly the same principal as if you were long a share and wanted to get out. For example, if the bid–offer price on Tesco is £1.75–£1.76, then to go short 1,000 shares sell at £1.75. An added bonus with short positions is that theoretically they can be held indefinitely; unlike say a futures contract which will always expire at some stage in the future.

The ability to go short stocks via CFDs also opens the doors up to many more trading strategies such as 'pairs' trading where two stocks from the same sector are bought and sold short simultaneously with the trader looking to capitalize on the price differential. For example, buying BP and selling short Shell, on the assumption that the BP share price will out perform Shell, in either an up or down market. Pairs trading will be discussed later on in the chapter.

No UK Stamp duty

When you trade a CFD you are not trading the physical stock, therefore the stamp duty levy is not applicable. Stamp duty like any charge is not so relevant for longer-term trading, but the impact that any cost has on short term trades is often critical. The lack of stamp duty on CFDs is a major boost, especially for short-term traders where the charge of 0.5 per cent can often eat up a significant proportion of profits, and, of course, is added to any losing positions.

Increased Leverage

Leverage is like fire, it can be your best friend but also your worst enemy. CFDs allow you to leverage your account by a factor of between 5 and 10 times depending on the share involved. Theoretically £20k cash can control between £100k and £200k of nominal trading positions. We feel the best way to use leverage is to view it as a tap which doesn't always have to be turned on to the maximum. Use its power wisely and respect its power. Margin yourself up when you can control the risks, or perhaps have a trade with an asymmetrical risk/reward profile, that is a trade with a tight stop but a potentially large profit if right. Otherwise use leverage sparingly or even in some cases not at all. The simple reason why leverage can be such a problem is that all losses are multiplied significantly.

Hedging

Perhaps you have cash stocks invested for the longer term and realize that buying put options in order to hedge has severe limitations, (see Chapter 6 on Options. But CFDs' inherent ability to go short stocks allows them to be used to set up perfect hedges. For example, you might work for a large multinational and own their stock or have stock options. If you're unsure of your company share price due to potential market turmoil but, say, the terms of your stock options prevent you from selling at present, then simply sell CFDs short. And remember to use the flexibility that these kind of products offer. You might own 10,000 shares, with a perfect hedge being to sell short 10,000 shares via CFDs, but what about just hedging 50 or 25 per cent of the position? This can easily be accomplished by using CFDs.

DISADVANTAGES OF CFDS

Cost of Doing Business

This is one area that the many CFD brokers won't tell you about, and it is important for you to realize the impact that commissions will have on your account. The leverage that CFDs offer you comes at a very high price in relation to other leveraged products such as futures. These costs simply relate to how commissions are charged on CFD deals. Look at this example to explain it in more detail.

Examples

The cost of doing business with a future – the FTSE 100

- Say the future is priced at 4,000 which at £10 a point equates to a nominal amount of £40,000.

- Therefore if you go long 1 future at 4,000 you are theoretically controlling £40,000 of stock.
- The commission for this future deal, even at the high end of brokers' charges will be around £10.
- As a percentage of the £40k nominal amount the commission equates to 0.025 per cent.

The cost of doing business with CFDS

If you buy £40k worth of stock using CFDs you are trading a leveraged product, in that you've only had to put up 10 to 20 per cent of the nominal value. However, you will pay commissions on the *full* nominal value of the shares. Therefore at a likely commission rate of 0.25 per cent this equates to £100.

In this example while both CFDs and futures use leverage, the commission on the future contract is 90 per cent cheaper than the CFDs' charge. Or, the other way around the CFD trade costs you 900 per cent more. Ouch!

The commission factor – a harder look at a dark topic

Good trading is no different from running any business, you not only have to keep an eye on costs but you have to do your own sums and analysis in this area. If you save money on your cost of doing business, it goes straight to your bottom line.

Assume you have a £20k account and you're using CFDs to short-term trade the market, trades lasting 1–3 days. You regularly use 4–5 times leverage and so your average bargain size is £90k. Round turn commissions are levied at 0.25 per cent per side (buying and selling) will be £450 or an incredible 2.25 per cent of your account balance per trade! If you trade on average once a week over a year your commission bill will be over £23,000, well over 100 per cent of your initial account balance!

But cut the amount of leverage that you use in half, and now only trade once every fortnight. You'll still end up paying nearly 30 per cent on your initial account balance in costs per annum. Therefore, if you trade CFDs with full brokerage commissions you may find that you end up working for your broker, rather than the other way around.

CFDs, when charged at full brokerage, are therefore an incredibly expensive product with which to trade, and too many people get dazzled by the leverage that's on offer, the lack of stamp duty, etc., and then wonder why it's so hard to make money. Chances are it is the hidden cancer of commissions that is their undoing.

However, all is not lost, brokers are starting to cut deals with clients and this will likely accelerate over the next few years with brokers such as

E*TRADE offering excellent flat commission rates combined with purpose-built software and trading packages.

CFD BROKERS

CFD trading is no different from trading shares, and in most cases you will be trading at the equivalent cash price. CFD brokers fall into two distinct camps: those that charge full rate commissions and those similar to E*TRADE that charge a fixed flat rate commission. Traders interested in opening a CFD account would be well advised to make sure they fully understand the damage that large commissions have on account balances.

E*TRADE

We are big fans of any product or service that reduces the cost of doing business and creates competition for the often fusty service traders get in London. We've been using E*TRADE for trading CFDs since late 2002 and have found that they offer the most competitive commissions of any CFD broker in London. They aren't just CFD brokers, clients can trade or invest in cash stocks and other financial products via their website, whilst their CFD and Forex trading platform allows the ability to work stop loss orders. Their backup and software platform sets the benchmark for the CFD world, offering real-time prices, charts and news as well sophisticated online account management capabilities. For further details go to their website at www.etrade.com .

OTHER CFD POINTS

Dividends

When a stock goes ex-dividend long holders of CFD positions will receive 80–90 per cent of the gross dividend value. This will be paid to you from the CFD broker in the form of a cash credit to your account, not via a cheque from the company as you would if you owned the cash stock.

If you have a short position in a stock and the share price goes ex-dividend, then you will be liable to pay 100 per cent of the gross dividend that will be debited by your broker from your account. On face value this doesn't look like good news for the short seller, but actually it doesn't really matter because when a stock goes ex-dividend the share price always falls by a similar amount. If you are short LloydsTSB and it pays a dividend of £0.05 per share then the share price will also drop by around £0.05 on the ex-dividend date. So although your account will be debited cash, the open short position will also benefit via the drop in the share price.

Shareholder rights

A CFD contract means that you don't actually hold the shares, you have in effect entered into an 'over the counter' (OTC) transaction with your broker. Therefore you will not receive any company communiqués, nor will you be able to vote or have any of the other rights of a normal shareholder. Rights issues are a different matter and long CFD holders are given the chance to subscribe to new shares under the issue, but these will again be issued in the form of a CFD contract, not the actual underlying stock.

How to deal

Dealing CFDs is as simple as dealing in cash stocks. You decide how many shares you want to trade, long or short, and what price you want to deal at. If you use a broker with good online software such as E*TRADE then you will see the bid–offer on your screen and, unlike spread bets, you will be able to get inside the spread. For example, say you want to buy 1,000 BSkyB and the market is £6.02–£6.06, you can easily place a bid of £6.04. The advantage of this process with online software is that you can play around with the bid–offer easily and effectively. Place a bid, reduce it, cancel it, move it up, etc., all without having to bother your broker via a tedious telephone call.

Beginners and CFDs

The other reason we prefer doing business with E*TRADE is that you can trade as little as one share using CFDs. If you are new to CFDs and want to gain experience or perhaps you're a little unsure of how to short trade effectively, then starting small is often a shrewd move. In fact, we would estimate that many private clients suffer early on in their trading careers because they simply trade positions that are too large. Trade small, learn the ins and outs of real-time trading, and then increase your size with the confidence and experience that you can only gain over time. Another advantage of E*TRADE is that they offer their software on a free 21-day trial using live prices. You can place trades, long or short in order to get a feel for what CFDs and the trading process are all about without actually committing any money.

When to use CFDs

CFDs are really tools for speculation and as with most margined products the best time to use them is when you expect swift, sharp moves to occur in the market. CFDs are not really designed to be investment products holding stocks for long periods of time, although because short CFDs pay interest there is no reason why they can't be held for the long term.

The ideal trade using a CFD would be when you expect a stock to move by 5–10 per cent within a week or so, before quickly taking your profit. You therefore want to be looking to trade in volatile stocks with good volume and tight bid–offer spreads, remember then the cost of dealing is inherently cheaper.

Pairs trading using CFDs

A 'pair' is two CFD positions, one taken out long and the other short in related products. Buying £5,000 worth of Vodafone while simultaneously selling £5,000 worth of British Telecom would be a classic example of a pair trade. Remember though that you want the monetary amount of both shares to be around the same level, so you wouldn't trade 1,000 shares of each unless the share price of the two shares was very similar.

The subtle point to realize about pairs trading is that you are effectively taking the underlying stockmarket direction out of the equation. You are simply trading the view that one share will outperform the other in either a bull or bear market. Take the Vodafone/BT example above. If the FTSE 100 index rises 25 per cent over a period of months then it is highly likely that both share prices will also rise, but is it likely that they'll *both* rise by 25 per cent to match the index? Say you buy Vodafone and sell short BT, Vodafone may well outperform the index rising 30 per cent, with BT under performing the index, rising only 20 per cent. In this case the 'spread' or price differential between the two shares would increase and the pair strategy would make excellent money.

Example

Simple Pairs Strategy Utilising CFDs

- Buy 4,200 shares of Vodafone at £1.20 (nominal value £5,040).
- Sell short 2,500 shares of BT at £2.00 (nominal value £5,000).
- FTSE 100 index rises 25 per cent.
- Vodafone shares rise 30 per cent to £1.56.
- BT shares rise 20 per cent to £2.40.
- Profit on Vodafone long CFD = £1,512.
- Loss on BT short CFD = (£1,000).
- Profit on deal = £512 (cost of doing business excluded).

But why not just buy the Vodafone shares outright? Because again, this pair strategy is not a bullish trade on either Vodafone or the stockmarket, and it is possible to make money whether the overall stockmarket goes up or down, as is highlighted below.

Example

- Buy 4,200 shares of Vodafone at £1.20 (nominal value £5,040).
- Sell short 2,500 shares of BT at £2.00 (nominal value £5,000).
- FTSE 100 index *falls* 50 per cent.
- Vodafone shares fall 40 per cent to £0.96.
- BT Shares fall 60 per cent to £1.20.
- Loss on Vodafone long CFD = (£1,008).
- Profit on BT short CFD = £2,000.
- Profit on deal = £992 (cost of doing business excluded).

To sum up, when you utilize a pair trading strategy such as this, you're trading the price differential between two shares with the overall market direction becoming almost irrelevant. However, you can still be very flexible with a pair strategy and trade them with a bullish or bearish market skew. If bullish instead of trading each side of the pair in the same nominal amount you could go long £3,000 of one share and short £2,000 of another, and vice versa for a pair trade that has a bearish skew.

Another twist using pairs

How about a sector to outperform or under-perform the actual index? Perhaps you're bullish on the mining sector but unsure on the overall direction of the FTSE 100. You could therefore buy £5,000 of CFDs on mining stocks and sell £5,000 of CFDs on the FTSE 100 (or you can use FTSE futures). Again the overall market direction of the FTSE 100 is being neutralized. If FTSE rises 25 per cent, this trade is expecting the mining sector to rise by more than 25 per cent. And whatever the FTSE may decline by, the trade is expecting the mining sector to fall less in percentage terms.

Example

- Buy £5,000 of Anglo-American shares using CFDs.
- Sell short £5,000 of FTSE 100 Index CFDs.

In 3 months time the FTSE has fallen 18 per cent, but Anglo-American has fallen only 10 per cent.

- Loss on Anglo-American = (£500).
- Profit on FTSE = £900.
- Profit on deal of £400 before costs.

And as in the Vodafone/BT pair this mining/FTSE pair can still be traded with an overall bullish or bearish skew by overbalancing either the long or short side of the trade.

When should you trade pairs?

First, traders who are new to these kinds of strategies should proceed with caution because we can assure you that there are twists and turns that you will not have considered, or surprises that the market will throw at you. The concept of pairs trading is relatively simple but their application in real-time trading is often a different matter. Pairs trading is all about relationships between two connected instruments and it is these inter-market relationships that can often be perverse. So do your own research, practice by paper trading or trading in small size where adverse moves won't affect your account balance too much.

Trading pairs on an everyday basis is normally a tough way to make your account grow for the simple reason that the relationships are fickle. But the best time to get involved with trading pairs is when the markets become volatile moving share prices to extreme levels. Then there's often good money to be made from trading shares whose price relationship is out of kilter. A good example of this would be some of the UK insurance stocks in the last half of 2002. These stocks were sold heavily down to extreme levels and the switched on pair trader would have been looking to buy the shares and sell the FTSE 100 short. Whatever the trade, it's volatile markets where pair strategies work best.

Create your own hedge fund using CFDs

Hedge funds were originally vehicles that created a balanced fund in the stockmarket, hopefully buying stocks in the best performing sectors while shorting stocks in sectors that were likely to under-perform. Most present day hedge funds do little of this style of trading.

But traders can easily create their own balanced fund using CFDs with their ability to go short the market. They can use fundamental or technical reasons to pick the stocks or sectors and with being both long and short they are effectively taking the overall direction of the stockmarket out of the equation. It is also a low risk form of investing especially when diversification is used to spread a portfolio over many unrelated sectors. An investor, for example, may chose to go long utilities, food retailers and energy while short telecoms, general retailers and banks. And as we have seen with the pairs trading a portfolio can also be skewed to be bullish or bearish by overloading one side. For example, if mildly bullish the overall market an investor could buy £50k of stock while shorting £30k.

However, with long CFDs the daily interest charge has to be considered within the overall context of costs. If the investor is looking to hold the shares for many months then it would be cheaper to go long stocks in the cash market rather than using CFDs because of the interest charges that are levied. The short positions can only be traded via CFDs but they carry the extra bonus of interest being credited to your account.

→ summary

CFDs are on the whole excellent vehicles to use for both speculation and investment purposes, but you must understand that because they use leverage they can be lethal if not treated with respect, which normally translates back to approaching your trading from the risk angle rather than simply looking to make money. Make sure you find a good broker when dealing CFDs with online software and a good commission schedule because if you pay higher dealing charges it is often tough to make money. And like trading any new product, start out small first before gaining the all-important confidence and experience.

6

Traded options

NO OBLIGATION

Aunt Agatha has passed away. You are waiting for probate on her will. By selling your existing house and with the money she has left you, you can buy the house you always wanted. But there is the risk that your house may not sell quickly or the lawyers may take their time. In the meantime your dream house might be sold or its price may rise out of your league.

You judge it to be a reasonable chance that you will have the money from both Aunt Agatha's will and your house sale within three months. You make the vendor of your dream house an offer: that if you pay him £5,000 today he sells you the right to purchase the house within an agreed three-month period for an agreed price, say £500,000. For a premium of £5,000 you have bought a call option that gives the right but imposes no obligation to buy the house at an agreed price and agreed time.

If the shares in Aunt Agatha's portfolio collapse or the sale of you own house falls through there is no obligation on you to buy the new house. However, you lose the £5,000. On the other hand, if the vendor is offered £550,000 for the house in the three months he cannot sell it. He is bound to sell it to you for £500,000.

For you, the £5,000 premium is not unlike an insurance premium. It becomes a sunk cost, it is not a deposit, it is not recoverable if the deal falls through. You might say you have insured yourself against the risk of not being able to buy the house. Conversely the vendor has insured against your not being able to buy the house, and whether you end up buying it or not he keeps the £5k.

These are the basics of an option and a demonstration of why options are not a new-fangled tool; they have been around for as long as people have been trading.

Financial options are an extension of this principle into the markets giving investors a tool that can be used in a myriad ways. This chapter describes options, the mechanics of using them and some strategies you can adopt to protect capital, earn extra income and for pure speculation.

A key element in the options market is volatility. Volatility is a measure of the range that the price of the underlying security is expected to fluctuate over a given period of time. Many people start speculating with options before they have grasped what option volatility is and how to use it. Understanding volatility is *crucial* to a successful options strategy. We discuss it in some detail below once we have described what options are and how they work.

WHAT ARE TRADED OPTIONS?

An option is a derivatives contract on an underlying instrument. Options on London stocks are often referred to as 'Traded Options', but there is no difference between a traded option and an option. All option contracts work the same way; understand what a stock option is and you will also understand how an option on a commodity product works.

Options come in two primary forms: calls and puts, and as most readers of this book are interested in the stockmarket we will primarily be focusing on equity options.

- A **call option** gives the holder the right, but *not* the obligation, to *buy* a fixed number of shares of the underlying stock at a fixed price within a fixed period of time. For example: *Reuters Jun £2.00 call* – the buyer of this call option has the right, but not the obligation to buy 1,000* Reuters shares at £2.00 on or before the expiry in June.

- A **put option** gives the holder the right, but *not* the obligation, to *sell* a fixed number of shares of the underlying stock at a fixed price within a fixed period of time. For example: *BP May 2002 £5.00 put* – The buyer of this put option has the right, but not the obligation, to sell 1,000 BP shares at £5.00 on or before the expiry in May.

An option only has a value for a fixed period of time. It is therefore known as a 'wasting' asset because its value can decrease or 'waste away' the closer it gets to the expiration date.

An option is also a security, just like a stock or bond, and constitutes a binding contract with strictly defined terms and conditions. All trading in exchange-based options, such as those on the London International

---

* There are around 90 UK equity options on LIFFE and all contracts are based on 1,000 shares apart from AstraZeneca which is for 100 shares.

Futures Exchange (LIFFE) or European Exchange (EUREX), are regulated by government bodies like the Financial Services Authority (FSA).

OPTIONS ARE FLEXIBLE

All options contracts on recognized exchanges (like all securities) are always tradable which means buyers and sellers are not locked into a contract until the expiry date. You can buy an option one minute, before selling it the next, or keep the position open for many months.

BASIC TERMINOLOGY

- *Premium*   The value of an option and what the buyer of the option pays.
- *Strike price*   The price at which the underlying product will be exchanged.
- *Expiry*   The date when the option will expire.

The same terminology applies to both call and put options as illustrated in the following examples.

Example

Vodafone Mar £1.30 call priced at £0.15

- The *premium* of the option is £0.15.
- The *strike* price is £1.30.
- The *expiry* is the third Wednesday in March.*

Tesco Jun £2.50 put priced at £0.70

- The *premium* of the option is £0.70.
- The *strike* price is £2.50.
- The *expiry* is the 3rd Wednesday in June.*

---

* LIFFE equity options always expire on the third Wednesday of the month. LIFFE index options on the FTSE 100 expire on the third Friday of the month.

HOW AN OPTION IS PRICED

An option is always priced in points or as some people call them 'ticks'. The point value is then multiplied by the 'tick size' to give the nominal cash value of the option. For example UK equity options on LIFFE are multiplied by a fixed £10 per point, so a call option on ICI trading at £0.21 or 21 points is worth £210.

You can also work out the value of an equity option by multiplying the option premium by the number of shares that one option contract represents. We have just seen that an option on UK stocks is on 1,000 shares, so with the same example as above, the ICI option priced at £0.21 is worth £0.21 × 1,000 shares, or £210.

Options on US stock always represent 100 shares, so a Microsoft $50 call priced at $0.50 is worth $0.50 × 100 shares, or $50.

Intrinsic and time value

There are always two components to the pricing of an option: *intrinsic value* and *time value*.

Intrinsic value

Intrinsic value is the price difference between the underlying security and the option's strike price. For example, using the BT Jun £2.00 call. If BT stock is at *any* price above £2.00 the call option has to be worth at least that difference. Therefore if the stock is trading at £2.46 the option will be priced at a minimum of £0.46. This should be easy to understand because if the option gives the holder the right to buy shares at £2.00 he or she can then immediately sell the shares in the cash market for a profit of £0.46. The reason why the option may well be worth more than £0.46 is because it has plenty of *time value* left.

If BT's stock price is £2.00 or lower then the option will have *no* intrinsic value. An option must be *in-the-money* (see below) to have an intrinsic value.

Time value

Time value is the amount by which the premium (price) of an option exceeds its intrinsic value. If the BT June £2.00 call is trading at £0.45 with the stock at £2.20 then the option will have time value of £0.25 and intrinsic value of £0.20.

If the BT June £2.00 call was valued at £0.10 with the stock price at £1.80 then there would obviously be no intrinsic value in the options and the £0.10 premium would all be time value. The longer the option has till expiry the more time value it will have and therefore the higher its price will be. If BT stock is trading at £2.00, the £2.30 call option with a month to expiry may well be trading at £0.05, but the £2.30 call with nine months till expiry is priced at £0.25. This is because within one month it is a lot harder for BT to rally over £0.50 than it is over a nine-month period.

An options value always equals *Intrinsic value + Time value*

AT-THE-MONEY OPTIONS – IN-THE-MONEY OPTIONS – OUT-OF-THE MONEY OPTIONS

There are three different terms used to describe both call and put options: 'At-the-money', 'in-the-money' and 'out-of-the money.' We will use the BT June £2.50 call as an example. Remember that this option gives the holder the right but not the obligation to buy BT stock at £2.50 on or before the June expiry.

- If the BT share price is greater than £2.50 the option will be referred to as 'in-the-money' because it has an intrinsic value.
- If the BT share price is less than £2.50 the option will be referred to as 'out-of-the-money' because its premium will consist only of time value.
- If the BT share price is at £2.50 the option is 'at-the-money'.

The thinking is obviously reversed with put options. Taking the BT June £2.00 put as an example:

- If the BT share price is less than £2.00 then the June £2.00 put will be 'in-the-money' and will have an intrinsic value.
- If the BT share price is greater than £2.00 then the put option will be 'out-of-the-money' and its premium will consist only of time value.
- If the price of BT stock is at £2.00 then the option will be 'at-the-money'.

THE RIGHT BUT NOT THE OBLIGATION

When describing options the word 'obligation' comes up time and again, so what exactly does it mean?

Example

Example using the Vodafone Jun £1.40 calls

● Vodafone stock is trading at £1.20.
If a trader buys this option then he has the right but not obligation to buy 1,000 Vodafone shares at £1.40 on or before the June expiry. So although the holder has the *right* to buy shares, he is not *obliged* to use it. If the share price remains below £1.40 before or on expiry then there would obviously be no point in electing the right to buy shares.

 FIVE COMPONENTS THAT AFFECT THE PRICE OF AN EQUITY OPTION

1 The price of the underlying stock versus the option strike price

The primary influence of an options premium is the price of the underlying security. Out-of-the-money or at-the-money options will have NO intrinsic value just time value. In-the-money options will therefore always be more valuable.

2 Type of option – put or call

Whether the option gives the right to buy the share or the right to sell the share.

3 The expiration date

An option will always expire at a known date in the future and the longer it has to expiry the more the option will be worth. For example if the March £1.20 Vodafone call is priced at £0.10, the December £1.20 call may be quoted at £0.25 because the share price has far more time over which it can move higher.

4 Volatility

The volatility part of the option pricing model is a measure of the range through which the underlying security is expected to fluctuate over time. The measurement of volatility is the standard deviation of the daily price changes in the security. The more volatile the underlying security or the perceived volatility, the greater the price of the option. So in effect options, both puts and calls, on stocks in the telecom sector will normally be far more expensive than options on shares in the drinks sector. Volatility is discussed in more detail below.

5 Interest Rates

Interest rates are a factor in the pricing of an option but they are not nearly as significant as volatility or the underlying share price. For the sake of simplicity, interest rates are not really worth bothering about; just take the view that the option professionals have priced in all known factors.

OPTIONS AND MATHS

Whereas in the general stock market maths does not play a particularly big role, in options it does. The pricing of options is always based on a series of mathematical calculations using such pricing methods as the Black–Scholes model. But is it necessary to get bogged down in all the analysis especially if maths has never been your strong point? There is, of course, no right answer; it all depends on how you view your own trading and analysis process. But traders who do want a more analytical approach should look into this topic further. There is an excellent free program designed just for this at www.hoadley.net and we would advise all options users to download it.

Ultimately though, what will make or lose you money with options is not how much theory you know, how intelligent you are or even how much money you have in your account. What will be the decider is simply your view on the underlying market and this is where you should spend at least 80 per cent of your research. If having a great mathematical mind was the solution to options trading then the average trader wouldn't stand a chance against the quantitative analysts and so-called rocket scientists, and while there is certainly evidence to state that some of these people do make a lot of money, there have also been many examples of where they've crashed and burned. The most famous being the destruction of Long Term Capital Management in 1998 which lost about $4 billion or 90 per cent of their capital in little over six months. The principals of this fund were a mixture of Nobel Prize laureates, PhDs, university boffins, economic wizards, etc. and were once regarded as the most talented bunch of market participants ever assembled. The reason for their downfall was simple, it was a combination of being too clever in thinking that their mathematical models had taken into account all possible variables of potential market movement, alongside using too much leverage.

EUROPEAN/US STYLE OPTIONS

When dealing in options there are two styles, European and US. Confusingly the terms have nothing to do with the different continents.

European style options can only be exercised on the day of expiry. For example if you owned the IBM June $65 call with the shares at $75, you can't exercise this option and receive the shares until the expiry day. Of course, you will still be able to freely trade the option in the marketplace.

US style options can be exercised at any time on or before expiry. If you owned the Abbey National Dec £5.00 with the shares at £6.00 you could exercise the option and take delivery of 1000 shares at anytime before the December expiry date.

All options on UK equities are US style and are therefore more flexible. Although they trade both the US and European style options on the LIFFE FTSE 100 index, most, if not all, of the business is done in European style. Where you have a choice between the two always try and trade the ones where there is more liquidity and volume.

OPTION VOLATILITY

Volatility is the most overlooked and *dominant* factor of option trading. Volatility affects the price of an option today and its price in the future. At the beginning of this book we mentioned that a lot of people lose money trading simply because they either don't fully understand what they're doing or don't have a solid grounding in the products that they're trading.

Trading without understanding the impact that volatility has, is just one reason why many people get substandard results when dealing in options.

Think of volatility in terms of car insurance. Car insurance is simply about risk so a 25-year-old wanting to insure a Porsche will incur a dramatically higher premium than a 50-year-old. If you were the insurance company, would you not demand a higher premium for doing business with the 25-year-old? Translate this example into options: the high risk 25-year-old is a telecom share, with the low risk 50-year-old is a utility share like British Gas. Or to look at it another way, what is the chance of a share in the telecom sector doubling or going broke within a year compared with a staid utility company?

How is volatility measured?

The measurement of volatility is shown as a percentage. If option volatility of the FTSE 100 is 20 per cent and the index is at 4,000, the options market is expecting FTSE to fluctuate between a range of 3,200 and 4,800.

If a stock is priced at £2.00 with a volatility level of 50 per cent the market is suggesting that the stock will fluctuate between £1.00 and £3.00. It is important to understand that this is not a forecast as to the future direction but rather an indication of the kind of moves either up or down that are likely to occur.

What you must never forget about option volatility is that it is always changing and today's reading may differ markedly from that of the future. When trading options your view on the future direction of volatility is sometimes far more important than your forecast for the underlying product as we will see.

Two types of volatility

Option volatility comes in two forms, historical and implied. Historical volatility is derived from past data, usually the previous 20 or 30 daily closes, while implied volatility takes into account not only what has happened in the past but also takes a view on the future. Imagine that there was going to be a general election tomorrow between two parties, A and B. If party A were to win then the stockmarket would likely gap higher by 15 per cent. If in the weeks leading up to the election there was no clear indication of the outcome there might be little movement in the stockmarket as it was waiting for the result. Historical volatility would decline because of the lack of movement. But implied volatility would remain very high because of the potential for a major move in stocks once the election result was known. If you're using volatility you should pay more attention to the implied volatility rate.

Don't worry too much about the intricacies of the different types of volatility or how they are calculated. What is important is to keep things simple, understand volatility and always be aware at what level it is trading, especially if at historically high or low levels.

The effect that volatility has on an option price

Example

Assume that both Colt Telecom and Tesco shares are both trading at £1.00. The prices for the same option may well look like this:

- Tesco 3 month £1.25 call – £0.05.
- Colt 3 month £1.25 call – £0.20.

Both option strikes are 25 per cent out-of-the money but why is the Colt option worth 300 per cent more than the Tesco one? Because the underlying volatility of Colt is significantly higher than Tesco's volatility, and with the risk of price movement (either up or down) being higher so is the option price.

All options on volatile markets or stocks will inherently be more expensive than options on non-volatile stocks or products. However, volatility levels can change both in the short and the long term and the trader who disregards or doesn't take it into account is likely to struggle even if their views of the overall market direction are sound.

Changing volatility

A good way to look at the significance that volatility plays in the pricing of options is the following example.

Example

On the 21 September 2001 (following the New York tragedy) trader John wanted to buy the FTSE 100 index feeling that it was far too low. On the exact low of the move with the index at 4,220 he bought one Dec 4,800 call for 350 points, or £3,500 per contract.

John's forecast that FTSE was heavily undervalued couldn't have been better and by the option expiry date of 21 December 2001 the FTSE 100 index stood at 5,100, a massive gain of nearly 21 per cent. However, the Dec 4,800 call was now only worth 300 points or £3,000, and therefore a loss of £500 was recorded on the trade. How can this be right? John did everything by the book, he bought a call, which *always* make money when the underlying rises.

But textbook theory, as shown in this case, doesn't always play out perfectly. The reason why he lost money was that he bought an option when volatility was at a historically high level, meaning that all options whether puts or calls were priced at very high premiums. He therefore ended up fighting a battle on two fronts, that of direction of the market which he got spectacularly right, but also a battle against falling volatility which was his downfall. The profits on direction were more than eaten up by the losses caused by volatility shrinking, hence reducing the premium of his option. It was as if everyday the market went up the price of his option gained by 10 points, but then volatility shrunk taking 11 points away. Figure 6.1 shows you the FTSE daily chart of this example.

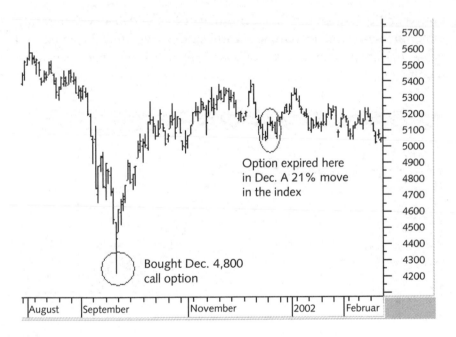

Figure 6.1

Recent and current volatilities

In order to get a better feeling for option volatility look at the levels for a selection of shares in 2002. You can see from the table that for the first six months of the year volatility either did not move much or went lower, and this was to be expected because the stockmarket traded in a tight range for the first five months of the year. But with the falling prices of early summer volatility made some dramatic moves higher and therefore option premiums went higher across the board.

	Feb	Apr	2002 early July	Oct	Dec
Alliance & Leicester	32%	20%	27%	46%	28%
Allied Domecq	25%	16%	25%	42%	26%
P&O	37%	31%	32%	50%	37%
Vodafone	34%	42%	63%	74%	45%
FTSE 100	17%	15%	31%	46%	27%

Low volatility was evident for the first half of 2002 and then with the sharp move down in the index starting in early summer, volatility exploded and hence option premiums both calls and puts, became very expensive (Figure 6.2).

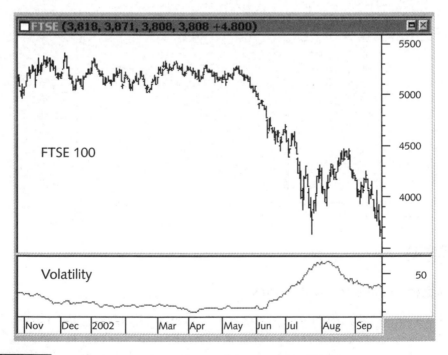

Figure 6.2 Twenty-day historical volatility of FTSE 100 cash

Where to find implied volatility?

- Your broker.
- LIFFE daily sheets for UK equity options – published online by 6.30pm, see www.liffe.com .
- Technical analysis packages such as Metastock.

Unless you have the software to help you determine volatility levels your first port of call should be your broker. He will have quick access to this information but if you find your broker doesn't know what you're talking about, then get one that does. Options are a specialist subject and having a broker who understands them is all important.

Guidelines for FTSE volatility

One of the most important facts about volatility is that it will always, at some stage in the future, revert back to its mean. Therefore it never stays high or low indefinitely. Realize also that markets and individual shares do change in character over time and therefore historic levels of high and low volatility can change over the years. An example of this would be UK equities from 1990–1995 and then 1996 to present. What was considered a high volatility reading for a share in 1994 may well now be considered fairly valued.

You should also be aware that one reading of volatility is pretty useless unless you find the range of what is perceived to be expensive or cheap. It is therefore worthwhile to have this information at hand. For an important market such as the FTSE 100 the ranges of volatility shown below should be common knowledge for option practitioners. But what about finding the necessary information for a market or stock that you've never traded before? This is where your broker will come in. A quick phone call is all that's needed and the information that you're looking for is simple:

1   Where is volatility now?, and
2   What are the levels at which it is considered cheap or expensive?

Example

Volatility guideline for FTSE 100

Cheap – Under 20 per cent. 15 per cent is very, very cheap.
Fairly valued – 20–30 per cent.
Expensive – Over 30 per cent (Sep/Oct 2001 volatility peaked at over 70 per cent).

How to use volatility in your trading

In a general sense volatility moves higher as prices on the underlying decline. Conversely, as prices move higher volatility will tend to move lower. Basically most markets go down far more quickly than they move up or, to look at it another way, as price goes down prices become generally far more unstable and this is really the essence of volatility.

When trading or dealing options volatility should be your roadmap. If volatility is high then different strategies should be considered from when it's low. From p. 121 we list many different types of option strategies and state whether increases or decreases in volatility will help or hinder the trade in question.

Volatility summary

Ignore this topic at your peril when dealing in options. The majority of retail traders who deal in options haven't even heard of volatility let alone understand it. And then these same traders complain when 'strange' things happen to their option positions. The strange moves are normally caused by volatility moving thus inflating or decreasing option premiums, regardless of whether the stock or market is going up or down. To make money in options you can't just rely on your calling of the underlying, you have to think not only about the level of volatility today but also what it is likely to be in the future.

But as we've suggested here, to understand volatility and use it to your advantage doesn't have to be hard. An example of a simple rule to incorporate into your trading plan would be never to buy options when volatility is at high levels. Perhaps in a situation like this traders should consider a sensible policy of shorting options. Whatever your trading plan, the power and significance of volatility has to be respected.

OPTION TIPS

Options and expiry

Most options are never exercised, even if they are in-the-money on expiration. If a trader owns the BT Mar £2.00 calls and the stock is trading at £3.00 on or near the expiry date they could of course, elect to take delivery of 1,000 shares at £2.00. But more likely they would take the easy route and just sell the option in the market collecting the cash instead.

But some traders for whatever reasons do want to take delivery or deliver stock on or before the expiry day. In this case they would instruct their broker to exercise the options or they would automatically be exercised on expiry if in-the-money. To exercise options your broker will make sure that you have the necessary funds in your account beforehand, and while the delivery process sounds complicated, it is actually simple with the broker and the exchange handling all the necessary paperwork.

The importance of liquidity when dealing options

When trading any financial instrument, liquidity is critical. You want to conduct your business in markets with good volume and tight bid–offer spreads. A lack of liquidity basically means that you'll struggle to get a fair price when you enter and almost never when you want to exit in a hurry. It is a very subtle point with trading but more often than not the cost of doing business is the most crucial part of any trading plan.

But where do you find out about liquidity? The first thing you should do is check the average daily volume and the open interest on the options. Open interest in a derivative market is simply the amount of open positions presently available. For example, if you were long 10 call options on Vodafone and a colleague was short 25 calls, the open interest would be 35 contracts. The quick route to finding this information out is through your broker or via the LIFFE daily sheets available from www.liffe.com .

What you may well find is this. You have an idea that Whitbread will rise or fall significantly over the next few months and therefore with the leverage on offer, options seem the ideal trading vehicle. But then a quick check on the open interest in the options reveals that there are only 35 contracts outstanding which translates to total commitments on just 35,000 shares, clearly a miniscule amount when dealing with a company the size of Whitbread. In our opinion it is not worthwhile dealing because the bid–offer spreads will be very wide.

Your trading thoughts then turn to GlaxoWelcome shares, and this reveals an open interest of over 50,000 option contracts. You can therefore be sure that the bid–offers will be tight and trading liquidity will be good. But going back to the Whitbread example, if you can't deal in the options then what can you do to get some leverage? Simply use CFDs as discussed in Chapter 5.

What option strikes to use

An area with which many people struggle is which option strike to trade. If a share is at £1.00 and you're bullish, which call option should you trade: the £1.10, £1.20, £1.30 etc.? Unfortunately there is never 'one size fits all' type of answer. The first questions you must answer are: where do you think the share price is going and over what sort of time period? Then see what the volume and open interest is on the individual option strikes. What does the daily chart look like? Is the market trending? Is it in a range? All of these inputs will help you make a logical trading decision. Also, how bullish are you? If super bullish then look to trade further out-of-the-money options, but if only mildly bullish then nearer-to-the-money options.

What option months to use

Once you've worked out what strike or strikes to trade you now have the problem of what month to trade. Again, there are no right or wrong answers. Clues will again be offered via the open interest and volume. Always try and check these levels early on because when there are multiple months to choose from some months will hardly trade at all.

All options eventually expire so you must come up with some sort of time period for your trade. Perhaps you think the move will come within a month, perhaps it is a long-term move. One point that cannot be emphasized enough is this problem of timing. Chances are if you trade options with too little time value your market view is often correct but you'll end up losing money because the stock or market makes its move *after* the options have expired. For example, you buy the March Vodafone £1.30 call in February, but the stock doesn't start rising until April. It is therefore always good advice to buy the next month out, i.e. if you want to buy the January options, better to buy February. Yes, the longer dated options will cost you more but your percentage chance of being correct rises as well.

The correct way to choose your options

The best and only way to find the right combination of option strikes and months is to play around with what's offered. For example, it's Christmas 2002 and you're mildly bearish on the FTSE index over the next few months. The near months available are January, February and March 2003. The strikes between 3,925 and 3,525 look sensible with regard to your bearish view. So now you've got to play around with them. What would your P&L be if the FTSE went to 3,650 and you traded the Mar 3,775 series? What if you trade the Feb, or perhaps do a combination of the Feb and March, etc.? These calculations don't have to be complex and should be done quickly. Only by doing enough of them will you start to see which options are best for any individual trading idea. And as we've mentioned before the free software from www.hoadley.net does an excellent job with these types of calculations and analytical approach.

Option brokers

If you trade options then you should be dealing with an options broker, not a stockbroker who also offers the ability to trade options. There is a big difference. The execution of stock orders is simple but with options it is far more difficult because of the inherent lack of liquidity, etc. A good options broker knows this and will work to get you good prices, or perhaps suggest better strategies.

If you need advice on different brokers and which is best for your style of trading then go to one of the free broker advisor sites such as www.broker-advice.com . The options market is small and you need to trade with people who are directly involved in the market, who understand what their clients need and have the necessary back office to clear and margin the trades correctly.

Get tight on spreads

The inherently large bid–offer prices quoted for many options including the LIFFE equity options turns many retail traders off. Yes, the spreads are often wide but you have to realize that it's possible to tighten them up and get a fair dealing price. You might only save a point or two, but do this on every trade and that's a lot of money at the year end.

Option market makers generally quote wide prices because they follow far too many different options to be able to update their prices all the time. The wide bid–offer is therefore somewhat understandable. But they will normally quote a tighter price if a trader starts to quote against them. For example, say you're interested in buying an option that is quoted at 70 bid–80 offered. Of course, you can get a guaranteed fill if you pay the offer price of 80 but why not use some intelligence and play the game as it's supposed to be played. Make the assumption that you won't be able to buy below the mid-price of 75, so now you can tighten up the market to 75–80. But it's still unlikely that you'll buy at 75 because normally with all options you have to give the market maker a point or two. This point or two is basically the market maker's edge and in most circumstances he would sell his mother before giving it up!

So, in order to buy your option with the market currently 75–80, it would be good advice to bid 77 and see what happens. If no trade, then bid 78 and, finally, 79, where in most cases, apart from when the market is very volatile, you should get filled. This process seems complicated but if you have online software it's just the sort of game that all good option traders play. The moral here is to play with the bid–offer spread as well as with your competitors in the market, because that's what they're doing with you.

When to hit the bid or offer

There are, however, times when it's not a good idea to get too clever, and just trade at the market. When the underlying gets very volatile you are often best advised to buy or sell at the market. A lot of money has been lost over the years by people trying to get too clever and save a few points in situations such as this. As a rule of thumb always strive to get the best price in normal markets and when volatile deal at the market.

→ summary

In order to fully understand options and trade them successfully you've got to work at them. They can be hard to understand at first but in reality any options strategy can be understood by breaking it down into the individual options, seeing how they will perform as a result of different market outcomes and then building the strategy back up.

But don't fall into the trap in thinking that options will make you money if you study them enough, they won't. What will make you money is your view on the underlying share or index. It is therefore always good advice to spend at least 80 per cent of your time on researching the market and only 20 per cent on the best option strategy to use.

Learning by doing is probably the best advice with options. Making transactions, making mistakes, looking back at the volatility of the trades you have undertaken will probably teach you as much and give you as much of a feel for options as staring at a textbook.

Finally, never disregard the importance that volatility plays in the pricing of options. As we've mentioned time and again, let volatility be your roadmap when deciding what type of strategies you should be trading. If it is very high then you should lean more towards the selling or writing of options, if volatility is low then buying options can often pay large dividends.

OPTION STRATEGIES

The following is a list of the most common option strategies used in the markets today, along with ideas and tips about how to use and trade them. The diagrams used are called 'option payoff charts' and are sometimes useful to give a visual idea of the potential risk and reward. To use the grid correctly not only must you have a view as to market direction but also one on future volatility versus the present level.

Long call – bullish trade

For aggressive investors who are bullish about the prospects for a stock, buying calls can be an excellent way to capture the upside potential with limited downside risk.

RISK Limited.

REWARD Unlimited.

THE TRADE Buy an out-of-the-money call.

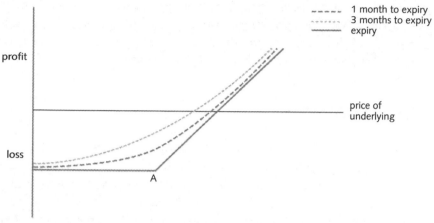

ABC stock at £5.00

Buy 1 Sep £5.50 call (A)

Source: Courtesy of liffe.com

WHEN TO USE You are very bullish on the stock. The more bullish you are, the higher the strike should be. No other position gives you so much leveraged advantage with limited downside risk.

VOLATILITY EXPECTATION Volatility bullish. Volatility increases greatly help the position, volatility decreases are a disaster.

PROFIT Unlimited in a rising market.

LOSS Limited to the initial premium, maximum loss if market expires at or below the option strike.

BREAKEVEN Reached when the underlying rises above the strike price, by the same amount as the premium paid to establish the position.

TIME DECAY This position is a wasting asset. As time passes, value of position erodes toward expiration value. If volatility increases, erosion slows, if volatility decreases, erosion speeds up.

LONG CALL IDEAS
- Be very cautious about buying options (puts or calls) in high volatility environments. Often you will be right on your direction but lose or make little money due to contracting volatility.
- If you do buy calls when volatility is high then try and take profits/losses quickly before a reduction in volatility starts to take effect on premiums.

- Your timing must be excellent when buying calls – you almost want to see the market move in your favour that day.

- Don't look to buy options with less than 30 days left to expiry – time erosion is at its highest. 30–60 days as a rule of thumb.

- Instead of buying one option and if wrong, letting it expire worthless, consider buying two options with the same monetary risk. If the two options reduce in value by 50 per cent then dump the position.

- Try and sell a portion of your position if the option doubles, then consider bring stop up to unchanged.

- Always assume that your timing will be off when buying calls and take this into account.

- Before you buy the option at least consider other strategies.

Selling naked puts – bullish trade

RISK Limited because the stock can't trade below zero. Although the risk is limited, the losses, should the stock fall dramatically, can be very severe.

REWARD Limited.

THE TRADE An at-the-money put or out-of-the-money put is sold.

ABC stock at £5.00

Sell or 'write' Jun £4.50 put

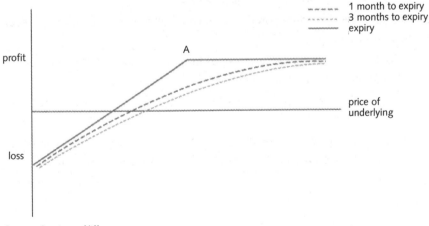

Source: Courtesy of liffe.com

WHEN TO USE You are neutral to mildly bullish on the stock. Sell lower strike options if you are only somewhat convinced; sell higher strike options if you are very confident the stock will stagnate or rise. If you doubt stock/index will stagnate, sell at-the-money options for maximum profit.

VOLATILITY EXPECTATION Bearish, increases in volatility hurt the position.

PROFIT Limited to the premium received from sale. At expiration, break-even point is strike price A less premium received. Maximum profit realized if stock settles at or above A.

LOSS Increases as stock/index falls. Because the risk is open-ended, this position must be watched closely.

BREAKEVEN Reached when the underlying falls below the strike price A by the same amount as the premium received from selling the put.

TIME DECAY This position is a growing asset. As time passes, the time value will shrink. Maximum rate of increasing profits occurs if the option is at-the-money.

NAKED PUT IDEAS
- Watch and *understand* the risk when selling puts naked
- Some short sellers of options will always cover and take the loss should the option premium double. If an option is sold at 50 points and it trades to 100, cover the trade immediately. This is excellent risk management advice.
- Good traders know what they're going to do before it happens – again, have a plan – don't hesitate.
- The best time to sell covered calls is when volatility is very high and the markets are very extended on the downside.
- Consider selling a position in pieces as your bullish view is confirmed – keep some powder dry.
- Consider covering the short option to take your profit when you collect 90 per cent of premium. If you sold it at 100, take profits at 10.
- Great way to accumulate cash stocks especially after a large fall when volatility is high.
- High seasonal tendency for stock markets to suffer large falls in Sep–Nov, therefore dangerous time to consider selling puts unless fully margined.

Covered call writing – bullish to neutral trade

Covered call writing is one of the most popular strategies for investors who own stock. A call option is sold short against a long stock position. It is an excellent strategy for bullish traders who want a nice low risk, limited return strategy. But there is a subtle twist with covered calls that all traders should understand. Trading covered calls is exactly the same strategy and associated P&L as selling a naked put. Some traders prefer to sell the put short because it's easier and the cost of doing business is cheaper because you don't have to pay two sets of commissions alongside the 0.5 per cent stamp duty.

RISK Limited.

REWARD Limited.

THE TRADE Buy cash stock, sell (usually) an out of the money call.

ABC stock @ £5.00

Buy 1000 ABC shares at £5.00, sell 1 Jun £6.00 call short

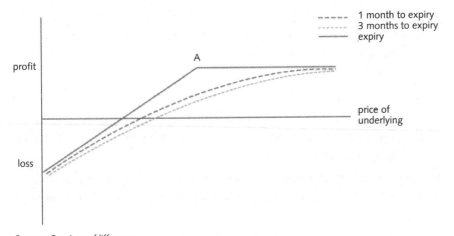

Source: Courtesy of liffe.com

WHEN TO USE You are mildly bullish or neutral towards a stock. The perfect result for this type of strategy is when the stock rises to the short call strike on expiration. If you bought the stock at £5.00, sold the £6.00 call short and then on expiry the stock price was at £6.00 you'd collect the entire premium from the option that expired worthless and keep the stock. Then, if you choose, repeat the process by selling another call.

Trading a covered call strategy also enables a trader to make a return in a flat market. If you bought the stock at £5.00, sold the £6.00 call and the stock was still around £5.00 on the expiry date, the short option would expire worthless so giving you a nice profit on the deal.

VOLATILITY EXPECTATION Volatility neutral to lower.

PROFIT Limited to the difference between the price where the stock was purchased and the short call option combined with the premium received from the short call.

LOSS Limited because the stock can't go below zero. Also if the stock rises considerably then the loss on the short call will be offset by the profit gained on the long stock.

BREAKEVEN Reached if the stock falls below the purchase price plus the option premium received.

TIME DECAY Time decay will help.

COVERED CALL IDEAS

- Consider 'legging' into them, buying the stock and selling the call on a rally in the stock price, therefore selling calls at a higher price and receiving more premiums if the share price rallies.

- Best to trade in slow upward trending markets.

- It's a bullish/neutral trade so can't really make money in a falling market. If prices do decline then the covered call writer will, however, lose slightly less than the holder of stock because he picks up the premium from the short options which expire worthless.

- Because you are collecting time value on the short options you want to try and sell options that have at least 3 months and preferably 6 months to expiry.

- Use charts to determine good levels to sell calls against.

- What happens if the stock blows through the short option strike? Nice 'problem' to have because you're still making money. If you think the stock price can hold or go higher then cover the short option and sell another out of the money call. If you think the stock is likely to slip back then keep the original short call.

- Using a short straddle is often a more conservative way of using trading covered calls. Instead of buying 2,000 shares and selling two call options, purchase 1,000 shares and sell an out of the money strangle, discussed on page 140.

- With LIFFE's introduction of single stock futures consider using them as a substitute for long stock, cost of doing business is cheaper but check the liquidity of the stock future beforehand.
- If you want to get leverage on these types of deals then use CFDs to establish the long stock position with their 5:1 gearing.

Call spread – bullish trade

Also known as debit spreads (you pay premium for them). Excellent strategy for bullish traders who want a nice low risk, limited return strategy.

RISK Limited.

REWARD Limited.

THE TRADE Buy a call, sell call at higher strike.

ABC stock @ £5.00

Buy 1 Jul £5.00 call (A), sell 1 Jul £5.50 call (B)

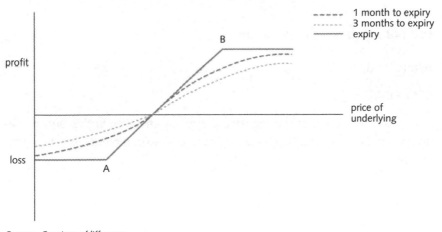

Source: Courtesy of liffe.com

WHEN TO USE You think the stock/index will go higher but without exploding on the upside. A very popular, bullish strategy.

VOLATILITY EXPECTATION Volatility neutral.

PROFIT Limited to the difference between the two strikes minus net premium cost. Maximum profit occurs where the underlying rises to the level of the higher strike or above.

LOSS Limited to any initial premium paid in establishing the position. Maximum loss occurs where the underlying falls to the level of the lower strike or below.

BREAKEVEN Reached when the underlying is above the lower strike by the same amount as the net cost of establishing the position.

TIME DECAY Time decay will hurt.

CALL SPREAD IDEAS
- Consider 'legging' into them, buying a call today and selling the higher strike call on a rally in the underlying.
- Often a better way to trade than buying outright calls, no explosive profit potential but far safer returns.
- Look to trade in trending markets.
- Always ask for the trade to be quoted as a spread rather than the two individual options.
- Be aware that if the underlying moves quickly in your favour, the spread might not gain too much, the full profit will be nearer the expiration date.

Bull put spreads – bullish trade

RISK Limited.

REWARD Limited.

THE TRADE Sell an out-of-the-money put and buy and even further out-of-the-money put. Since a put with a higher strike price is sold, the trade is initiated for a credit.

ABC stock at £5.00

Sell 1 Aug £4.50 put (B), buy 1 Aug £4.00 put (A)
or Sell Aug 1 £5.00 put, buy 1 Aug £4.50 put

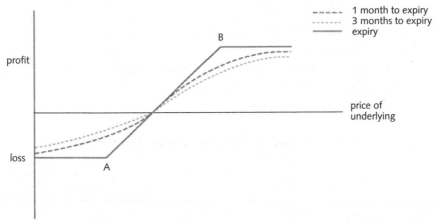

Source: Courtesy of liffe.com

WHEN TO USE Much the same as selling a naked put with the exception that you minimize your margin requirement and you limit your downside by purchasing a lower put strike price for protection. A good trade when you might not know where the market is going, but feel that it's unlikely to fall drastically. For example, you are neutral to slightly bullish/bearish.

VOLATILITY EXPECTATION Neutral.

PROFIT Limited to the difference between the two strikes plus net premium credit. Maximum profit occurs where underlying rises to the level of the higher strike or above.

LOSS Maximum loss occurs where the underlying falls to the level of the lower strike or below

BREAKEVEN Reached when the underlying is below strike the first strike by the same amount as the net credit of establishing the position.

TIME DECAY Time decay will help, you are selling time.

BULL PUT SPREAD IDEAS
● Look to initiate in 'dips' in a strong bull market or at the lower end of trading ranges.
● A good strike to sell is the at-the-money put or just outside-the-money, gives you greater time value.

Call ratio spread – bullish trade

RISK Limited.

REWARD Unlimited.

THE TRADE The trade itself involves selling a call (normally at-the-money or near-to-the-money) at a lower strike and buying a greater number of calls at a higher strike price. Depending on the strikes chosen, the position could also be established at breakeven or at a small premium cost.

ABC stock at £5.00

Sell 1 Jun £5.00 call (A), buy 2 Jun £5.50 calls (B)

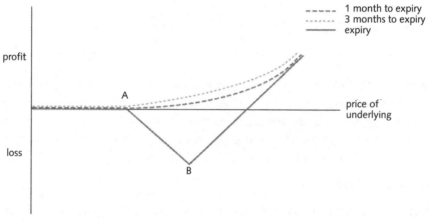

Source: Courtesy of liffe.com

WHEN TO USE For bullish investors who expect big moves in already volatile stocks/indexes, call back spreads are a great limited risk, unlimited reward strategy.

VOLATILITY EXPECTATION: Bullish, you want to see volatility levels keep at least stable, but preferably rise.

PROFIT Unlimited if underlying rallies.

LOSS Greatest loss occurs at higher strike which is the difference between strikes minus (plus) net credit (debit).

BREAKEVEN Lower breakeven point is reached when the underlying exceeds the lower strike option by the same amount as the net credit received (if initial position established at a net cost, there is no lower breakeven point). The higher breakeven point is reached when the intrinsic value of the lower strike is equal to the intrinsic value of the two higher strike options plus (minus) the net credit (debit).

TIME DECAY Hurts but not too much.

CALL RATIO SPREAD IDEAS
● Can use other ratios, two by three for example – sell 2 calls and buy 3 calls.
● Try and put on as near to zero price as possible, then good downside protection.
● Good trade to use when market has been rallying but has stalled into a trading range, and you expect a further breakout to the upside.

Long put – bearish trade

RISK Limited.

REWARD Limited because the stock cannot trade below zero. However, if the stock does sell-off dramatically then profits are likely to be huge.

THE TRADE Buy a put, the more bearish you are the further out-of-the-money, but be realistic. Perhaps look at a chart to get the character of the market.

ABC Stock @ £5.00

Buy 1 Jul £4.50 put (A)

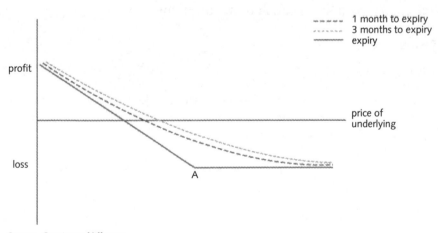

Source: Courtesy of liffe.com

WHEN TO USE Very bearish preferably in the short term. No other position gives you as much leveraged advantage in a falling stock/index (with limited upside risk).

VOLATILITY EXPECTATION Very bullish.

PROFIT Almost unlimited, assets cannot fall below zero.

LOSS Restricted to the premium paid.

BREAKEVEN Reached when the underlying falls below the strike price by the same amount as the premium paid to establish the position.

TIME DECAY This position is a wasting asset. As time passes, value of position erodes toward expiration value. If volatility increases, erosion slows, if volatility decreases, erosion speeds up.

LONG PUT IDEAS
- Consider mixing it up, maybe look to buy puts with different strikes.
- Watch that volatility. If the market has already tumbled then chances are that by going long puts you've missed the boat.
- If you're bearish try and buy them on rallies in a downtrend.
- Often a bad way to hedge stock risk because they are a wasting asset. For example if you are long ABC stock and buy a put and the share doesn't move lower you will lose money, and that's not hedging.

Selling naked calls – bearish to neutral trade

RISK Unlimited.

REWARD Limited.

THE TRADE Sell a call. Selling naked calls can be a risky strategy. It should be utilized with extreme caution in conjunction with a solid plan for reducing risk should the market move against you.

ABC stock at £5.00

Sell Jun £5.50 call

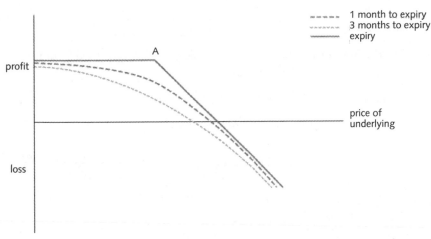

Source: Courtesy of liffe.com

WHEN TO USE You are sure that the price will not rise and/or expect lower volatility. Sell higher strike options if you are only somewhat convinced; sell lower strike options if you are very confident the index/stock will stagnate or fall. Sell at-the-money options for maximum profit.

VOLATILITY EXPECTATION Bearish, increases in volatility hurt the position.

PROFIT Profit is limited to the premium received and thus if the market view is more than moderately bearish, a long put may yield higher profits.

LOSS Unlimited in a rising market.

BREAKEVEN Underlying settles at strike plus premium received.

TIME DECAY This position is a growing asset. As time passes, value of position increases as option loses its time value.

NAKED CALL IDEAS
- Look to sell when a stock spikes especially when volatility is high.
- Great way to trade when the stock/index has already made a good move.
- Look at charts to get some market character.
- Have an *iron clad* plan for getting out if the market takes off.

Put spread – bearish trade

RISK Limited.

REWARD Limited.

THE TRADE Buy an at-the-money put, sell an out-of-the-money put. Your profits come as the stock/index drops.

ABC stock at £5.00

Buy 1 Jun £5.00 put (B), sell 1 Jun £4.50 put (A)

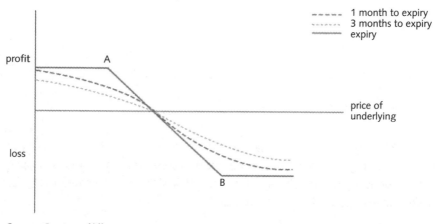

Source: Courtesy of liffe.com

WHEN TO USE You think the stock/index will go down somewhat or at least is slightly more likely to fall than to rise.

VOLATILITY EXPECTATION Neutral.

PROFIT Limited to the difference between the two strikes (minus net premium cost). Maximum profit occurs where underlying falls to the level of the lower strike or below.

LOSS Limited to the initial premium paid in establishing the position. Maximum loss occurs where the underlying rises to the level of the higher strike or above.

BREAKEVEN Reached when the underlying is below the long strike price by the same amount as the net cost of establishing the position.

TIME DECAY Hurts, but not nearly as much as a long put.

PUT SPREAD IDEAS

● Be two dimensional – the market is likely to move lower but not lower than this level.

● Consider 'legging' into them.

● Maybe put the trade on in half-size and then look to leg into the other half.

● Always ask for the strategy quote when dealing rather than the two options outright.

Bear call spread – bearish trade

RISK Limited.

REWARD Limited.

THE TRADE Sell a call, buy call at higher strike.

ABC Stock at £5.00

Sell 1 Jul £5.00 call (A), buy 1 Jul £5.50 call (B),
or Sell 1 Jul £5.50 call (A), buy 1 Jul £6.00 call (B)

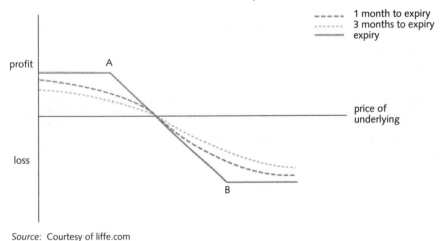

Source: Courtesy of liffe.com

WHEN TO USE Moderately bearish or expect at least sideways movement, remember you are selling TIME to benefit from natural time decay.

VOLATILITY EXPECTATION Neutral to bearish.

PROFIT The premium you receive upon opening the spread.

LOSS The difference between the two strike prices minus premium received.

BREAKEVEN Lower strike plus premium received.

TIME DECAY Helps.

BEAR CALL SPREAD IDEAS
● Good strategy for use in a trading range.

Long straddle – neutral, forecasting movement

RISK Limited, but should not really be viewed as a low risk strategy because you are paying out for two options which are wasting assets.

REWARD Unlimited.

THE TRADE Call option and put option are bought with the same strike – usually at-the-money.

ABC stock at £5.00

Buy 1 Jun £5.00 call (A), buy 1 Jun £5.00 put (B)

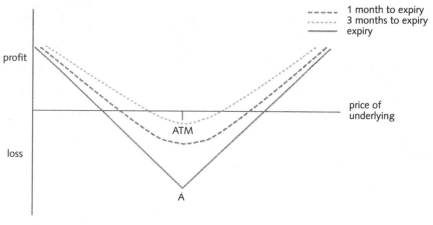

Source: Courtesy of liffe.com

WHEN TO USE You believe that the stock/index is about to make a large move in either direction. A good time to utilize straddles is where there has been a prolonged period of extreme quietness and implied volatility is around multiyear lows. If this is the case look to do longer dated months rather than the shorter ones. Spring 2002 in the FTSE 100 was a good example of the perfect market conditions.

VOLATILITY EXPECTATION Very bullish. Volatility increases improve the position substantially. Volatility should therefore be monitored closely.

PROFIT Unlimited for an increase or decrease in the underlying.

LOSS Limited to the premium paid in establishing the position. Loss will be greatest if the underlying is at the initiated strike at expiry.

BREAKEVEN Reached if the underlying rises or falls from option strikes by the same amount as the premium cost of establishing the position.

TIME DECAY Hurts a lot, remember you have double time erosion because of the two options bought. Decay depends a lot on volatility. If volatility increases time decay will decrease, etc.

LONG STRADDLE IDEAS
- Work best on stocks/indexes that are likely to move.
- Consider 'legging' into them – buying the calls today and buying the puts on a rally or vice versa.
- Always best to use some sort of time stop because of the time decay.
- If you're expecting a very large breakout then better to trade strangles discussed below.
- Are there any clues on the chart to consider liquidating the opposing option? You buy a straddle, market breaks out to the upside, then possibly look to sell the put.
- Very hard trade to make money on if you buy the options when volatility is high.

Long strangle – neutral but forecasting movement

RISK Limited.

REWARD Unlimited but should not be viewed as a low risk strategy, or to put it another way most long straddles and strangles expire worthless.

THE TRADE Buying out-of-the-money calls and puts.

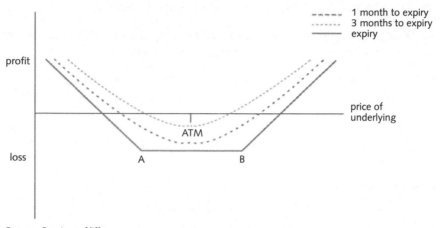

ABC stock at £5.00

Buy 1 Jun £6.00 call (A), buy 1 Jun £4.00 put (B)

Source: Courtesy of liffe.com

WHEN TO USE You believe the stock/index will have an explosive move either up or down. This strategy is similar to the buy straddle but the premium paid is less, but then a larger move is needed to show a profit.

VOLATILITY EXPECTATION Very bullish, increases in volatility work marvels for the position.

PROFIT The profit potential is unlimited although a substantial directional movement is necessary to yield a profit for both a rise or fall in the underlying.

LOSS Occurs if the market is static; limited to the premium paid in establishing the position.

BREAKEVEN Occurs if the market rises above the higher strike price at B by an amount equal to the cost of establishing the position, or if the market falls below the lower strike price at A by the amount equal to the cost of establishing the position.

TIME DECAY This position is a big wasting asset. As time passes, value of position erodes toward expiration value. If volatility increases, erosion slows, if volatility decreases, erosion speeds up.

LONG STRANGLE IDEAS
- Can mix the strikes up depending on whether you lean towards the bull or bear tract but are still overall neutral. Perhaps you feel the odds slightly

favour a bull move. If stock is at £5.00 instead of buying the £4.50 put and £5.50 call you could buy the £4.50 put and £6.00 call.

- Use some sort of time stop because time erosion is your enemy.
- If you expect a mega move then this is a better strategy than straddles because strangles are cheaper to buy and you can therefore buy more with the same amount of capital.
- Look to trade when market has been quiet for a long time and volatility is low, if this is the case look to trade the longer dated months.
- Look at the charts for any clues, if market is breaking out then maybe ditch the 'wrong' option.

Short straddles – forecasting no movement

RISK Unlimited.

REWARD Limited.

THE TRADE A short straddle is an option strategy in which an at-the-money call and an-at-the money put are sold. It is used to profit on a stock/index when little movement is expected in either direction.

ABC stock at £5.00

Sell 1 Jun £5.00 call, sell 1 Jun £5.00 put

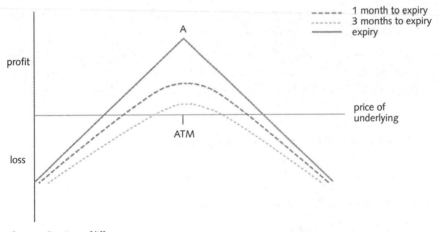

Source: Courtesy of liffe.com

WHEN TO USE For aggressive investors who do not expect much short-term volatility, the short straddle can be a risky, but profitable strategy. If you only expect a moderately sideways market consider selling strangles instead.

VOLATILITY EXPECTATION Bearish, volatility increases wreck the position.

PROFIT Limited to the premium received, highest profit when the market settles at the sold strike.

LOSS Unlimited for either an increase or decrease in the underlying.

BREAKEVEN Reached if the underlying rises or falls from sold strike by the same amount as the premium received from establishing the position.

TIME DECAY Helps, especially when the trade is initiated in periods of high volatility.

SHORT STRADDLE IDEAS
- Nice trade to put on after a big move on the expectation that things will quieten down.

- Maybe look to buy strangles with premium received – this would be for protection.

- Always ask yourself serious risk questions before you do this trade. Many people will say it is a dangerous trade but only if you don't know what you're doing.

- Consider starting to cover (reduce position) when 75 per cent of premium is collected or in the final month, remember short dated options will increase the most on sudden moves. If you sell the straddle for 200 points then start to take profits if it trades down to 50 points.

- Some sellers of straddles and strangles often use a simple stop; liquidate the entire position if the initial premium received gains by 50 per cent. So if you sold the strategy for 100 points, stop yourself out if it moves to 150 points.

Short strangle – forecasting a lack of movement

RISK Unlimited.

REWARD Limited to the option premium received.

THE TRADE Selling out-of-the-money calls and puts.

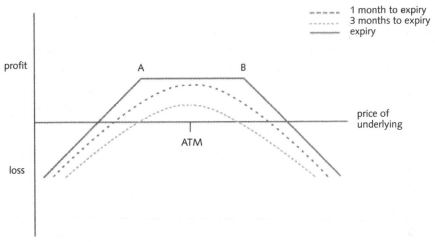

BT shares @ £3.00

Sell 1 Sep £3.50 call (A), sell 1 Sep £2.50 put (B)

- - - - - 1 month to expiry
· · · · · · 3 months to expiry
———— expiry

profit

A   B

price of
underlying

ATM

loss

Source: Courtesy of liffe.com

WHEN TO USE You believe the stock/index will move in a range or sideways type price action. This strategy is similar to the sell straddle but the premium received is smaller, but then a larger move either way is needed to show a loss. Which options to sell (or how far away from the underlying price) depends on what type of range you expect. Expecting a tight range, nearer-the-money. Expecting a wide range, then further out-of-the-money.

VOLATILITY EXPECTATION Very bearish, a decrease in volatility will work well for the position

PROFIT The profit potential is limited but a substantial and sudden move can turn this trade into a big loser especially if one of the sold options goes 'into the money'. But generally considered as a more cautious trade than a 'short straddle'.

LOSS Unlimited for a sharp move in the underlying in either direction.

BREAKEVEN Occurs if the underlying expires below strike A or above strike B by the same amount as the premium received in establishing the position.

TIME DECAY This position is a big wasting asset therefore time decay helps enormously. But if volatility increases, erosion slows, if volatility decreases, erosion speeds up.

SHORT STRANGLE IDEAS

- You can mix the strikes up depending on whether you lean towards the bull or bear tract but are still overall neutral. Perhaps you feel the odds slightly favour a bull move.

- A good stop level is if the strategy doubles in price (some also use a 50 per cent increase, maybe use a combination of both), i.e. you sell the strangle and receive 50 ticks and then buy it back on stop for around 100 ticks.

- Always have a strict risk plan beforehand and stick to it – remember one or two trades can wipe out a year's profits or even force you out of trading when dealing with short options.

- Look at the charts for any clues, if market is breaking out then maybe ditch the 'wrong' option.

7

Futures

ACCOMMODATING THE FUTURE

If you are a farmer growing wheat you can sell it when it is still germinating in the ground, you don't have to wait for the harvest once a year. There is an international market and price for grain and the price fluctuates throughout the year. If the price of wheat is strong in March and you are staring out across fields of green shoots, you can still take advantage of the high price. If you're an industrial baker making bread, you need to buy wheat throughout the year whatever the price. You would like a product that enables you to take advantage of low wheat prices today for delivery in the future.

Futures were designed to accommodate both the producers and users of a product. If the price of wheat is high in March then the farmer using futures can sell forward his harvest for delivery in September. He would do this by selling September futures short. If the bakery company uses 5,000 tonnes of wheat a month and if prices in its view are low in October, it can use futures to forward buy its production need. If the current month was October it would buy the December, March and June futures contracts in order to take delivery of wheat when those futures contracts expire.

Just a minor complication here. You have probably heard of forward contracts and wonder how they differ from futures, after all they are both for transactions to be completed at a future time. Futures contracts are standardized, exchange-traded contracts. Forward contracts, which we don't cover here, are customized, off-exchange contracts. If our farmer did a deal to sell his March wheat direct to the baker in September he would be by-passing any exchange and they could agree whatever amounts they chose. We would class that as a forward contract. However, whereas the credit risk in futures contracts is assumed by the clearing house that holds the margin, our baker and farmer would be totally dependent on each other's creditworthiness. Moreover, if one or other of them did not want to complete the contract there would not be ready and willing partners to take over the open contract. If they had used a futures contract on an exchange there would have been the volume and liquidity and others with whom they could conduct their business.

SO WHAT IS A FUTURE?

A future is a contract to deliver or take delivery of a standardized amount of an underlying product at a fixed date in the future. For example, if you were to buy one December gold future you are entering into a contract to take delivery of 100 oz of gold on the December expiry date. However, as we'll see most, if not all futures that aren't used for hedging purposes never go into the delivery process. One could picture the shock on the face of an oil futures trader who had forgotten to sell a futures contract when he is advised that a supertanker has docked with 250,000 barrels of oil! Needless to say most practitioners never see the products in which they trade futures and there are easy mechanisms for avoiding taking delivery.

Although the speculators who trade futures have no real interest in grain, oil or gold from a physical, industrial or commercial point of view, they are welcomed into the marketplace because they provide the crucial liquidity. Without the speculators, who may be long- or short-term players, then the farmers and bakers of the world would just be trading with each other. This would remove the opportunities for them to plan their production and cash flow, protect themselves against market volatility, or take advantage of market anomalies.

When people are first introduced to the workings of futures using commodities as an example they are often puzzled about how and why financial futures such as stock indexes came about. It is a good question because there are certainly no producers and consumers of stock indexes. But a fund manger will often use them to hedge or protect against downside stockmarket risk. Or he might buy stock market futures today at what he deems cheap prices because every month through pension additions he gets more money to allocate to the market and he wants to put that money to use today, although he won't receive it till some time in the future.

ARE FUTURES FOR YOU?

The ordinary retail investor probably does not fit the profile of a futures trader. Futures traders are either commodity professionals who are engaged in trading cocoa for Cadburys, wheat for Hovis or pork bellies for Walls. The financial futures traders are speculating or helping institutional investors with billions of pounds under management determine strategies for the acquisition or disposal of stock, minimizing the impact of volatility or leveraging to enhance the performance of a portfolio.

The semi-professional futures trader is perhaps someone who has made a lot of money in say, property, is a skilled market reader and thrives on the risks that futures offer. You will also tend to find that often the people making money trading futures are the ones that trade full time.

WEALTH WARNING

If your capital is less than, say, £25K, we suggest that you're probably better off trading a product like CFDs where you'll be in a far better position to watch your risk.

It's likely that the only reason somebody would consider futures is purely for speculation and in our opinion because of the inherent size of most futures contracts (one FTSE contract is worth around £40,000) most people are better off trading products such as CFDs or options where the smaller risk can be defined. Perhaps a sensible plan would be to get some experience in other leveraged products before attempting to trade futures.

But before you throw in the futures towel there is one attractive aspect of futures which may appeal to the ordinary investor: tracker funds have become very popular in recent years. They allow investors to track a particular index like the FTSE 100 without having to manage their investment. As we relate below, it is possible to create your own tracker fund using futures. Besides the attraction of not having to listen to the hype or explanations of a tracker fund manager (who doesn't actually have to manage anything) you can save a lot of money in the fees that keep him in the style to which he thinks he ought to be accustomed.

WHAT CAN YOU TRADE FUTURES ON?

Futures are available on almost any financial and commodity product from stockmarket indexes, currencies, individual stocks, softs such as cocoa and coffee, interest rates and bonds – even cheddar cheese! All futures work on the same principles – the only difference being whether they are physical, or cash settled. As a rule of thumb if you're dealing on a product that can be physically owned or touched such as a bond or sugar then it is normally physical delivery. But if it's on an index such as the FTSE 100 then it is cash settled, after all it's not possible to own or touch the FTSE 100.

Whether a future is cash or physically delivered it won't matter to 99 per cent of speculators because they are only interested in trading the movement of the underlying product. If a speculator has a position in a futures contract which is about to expire he will either 'roll' his position into the next trading month or cover the future in the market. A futures 'roll' is where, for example, a trader has a long position in the December contract which is about to expire, and so simultaneously sells December and buys March so 'rolling' his long position over. This is a very common trade around expiry time. If, however, he doesn't want to roll the position over he will just sell in the market to go what is referred to as flat (neither a long nor short position).

 ## HOW THE P&L OF A FUTURES CONTRACT WORKS

Contract size

One futures contract represents a specific quantity of an underlying commodity or product. For gold this is 100 oz, for crude oil it is 1,000 barrels, etc. For futures on an index this does not apply because you cannot physically own an index. The size of an index product is determined by the index level multiplied by the tick size discussed below.

Point or Tick size

A futures point is the minimum amount that a futures contract can move, and is often referred to as a tick. A tick will also represent a fixed monetary amount such as £10 for the FTSE contract. However, you must always check these facts because they can be ambiguous. In the case of the FTSE the minimum fluctuation is actually 0.5 of a point, or £5 but most traders will refer to a tick as 1 point or £10.

Examples

A simple example of a long futures trade – crude oil

- The contract for crude oil on the NYMEX Exchange (New York) is on 1,000 barrels of oil.
- The minimum tick is $0.01 and is worth $10. The tick value can always be checked against the contract size.
- If one crude oil future represents 1,000 barrels of oil then 1,000 × $0.01 = $10 a tick.
- Buy one contract to go long of December crude at $27.25.
- Sell the long position when the price moves up to $27.62.
- Profit ($27.62 minus $27.25) is $0.37 × $10 = $370 excluding commissions.
- Note taxes such as stamp duty are not applicable on futures contracts.

A simple example of a short futures trade – FTSE 100 index

- The contract size for the FTSE 100 index traded on LIFFE is the point value (£10) multiplied by the index value.
- A point is valued at £10.
- Sell short 1 March FTSE future at 4,050.
- Buy to cover short position at 4,100.
- Loss is therefore –50 points × £10 = –£500 excluding commissions.

MARGIN

The margin on a futures contract is dealt with in the same fashion as other types of margined products like CFDs and spread bets. There is an initial margin paid on all overnight positions and also the 'marked to market' variation margin debited/credited at the close of business every day.

The clearing house, an independent financial organization, sets the initial margin. While the initial margin stays pretty static over time, if the underlying contract gets very volatile, margins are normally raised. However, don't assume that just because the clearing house sets overnight margins at a certain price that this will also be the same level charged by your broker. It is not uncommon for brokers to insist on 1.5 or 2 times initial margin for certain products, such as the volatile stock indices. This is not such an unfair request because you will still receive interest on your monies that are used for margin purposes. In fact, over the long run it may be a subtle advantage to the trader because it will stop overtrading and taking on too much size in relation to the account size.

WHAT MONTHS TO TRADE?

All financial futures trade the quarterly months: March, June, September and December, with most if not all of the business being done in the front month, or the month nearest to the present date. If you're trading in February then the March contract will be the front month. If you see more than one month trading don't waste your time trying to work out which one to trade. Simply call your broker and ask him for guidance.

Each futures contract will have an expiry date, but before that will come the rollover period normally lasting a few days where all the positions that don't want to go into the delivery process are rolled into the next month. For example the FTSE 100 future always expires on the third Friday of the futures month. Assume that the date is now June. In the final week of the June future the volume in the next month September will start to creep up and by the Thursday the day before expiry, September will take over as the front month. This simply means that most of the volume will now be in the September. How will you know this information? Most traders rely on their broker to inform them when the date becomes near.

But what happens if you're trading in coffee futures, which are physically settled, and you forget to roll your long position over? You as a speculator are hardly in a position to accept delivery of hundreds of bags of Arabica coffee beans! Your broker knows this, and his back office will have many checks and safeguards in place to make sure that these events don't happen. Even if you're away on holiday, or are unconscious in hospital your broker will take the initiative and cover the position to make you flat before expiry. If you're trading in a cash settled product and forget to roll it, then it will just be settled against the expiry price and your account will be credited or debited the difference.

Example of cash settlement

- Buy 1 March FTSE 100 future at 4,000 a week before the expiry.
- Settlement (EDSP*) price of the March future is £4,075.
- The position is automatically settled against this price in a similar fashion as if you'd sold it on the market in the normal fashion.

WATCH THE LIQUIDITY OF A FUTURES CONTRACT

Just because there is a futures contract on a product, never trade it unless you first check the liquidity and open interest. Many futures contracts hardly trade, and you do not want to become involved with markets that have little volume or wide bid–offer spreads. Where do you find this information? Go to the Exchange website, or call your broker to check.

Open interest is the amount of 'open' contracts in existence. If you think about it, when a futures contract is first listed on an exchange, no traders will have positions. If you therefore buy 10 lots and someone sells 5 lots short then an open interest of 15 is created and so on. As a rule of thumb it is often good advice not to get involved in futures markets that have less than 10,000 lots of open interest and average daily volume throughout all the months.

SINGLE STOCK FUTURES/UNIVERSAL STOCK FUTURES

The London International Financial Futures Exchange (LIFFE) as well as the two US exchanges, One Chicago and NQLX now offer what are referred to as Single Stock Futures (SSFs) or Universal Stock Futures (USFs). Although the futures have different names they are the same products which are simply futures on an underlying stock. For example, you can trade a futures contract on Shell, Vodafone, Microsoft, etc.

* Exchange Delivery Settlement Price – This is the official settlement price of all cash settled futures contracts. For the FTSE 100 it is derived from taking an average of the cash index over a certain period of time (usually 15 minutes) on the day of expiry.

Although they have been listed on the LIFFE for about two years and were introduced on the American exchanges at the end of 2002 the volume and open interest has not yet been forthcoming. This is a good example of why looking into the liquidity issue is critical before you consider trading any futures contract. Don't assume that just because there is good business in the underlying product that the futures will be liquid and easily tradable.

The jury is still out on whether stock futures will take off, but a lot of traders are hoping that they succeed and gain liquidity because they offer a cheap and effective way in which to trade stocks with leverage. However these futures are suffering somewhat from the chicken and egg syndrome in that until the volume builds, traders will not commit capital to them.

For further information log on to the following websites:

www.liffe.com
www.nqlx.com
www.onechicago.com

LIMIT UP AND LIMIT DOWN – TRADING HALTS

Some futures, notably those on commodities, and most futures based in the US have what is called a daily or intraday limit. A limit move is the maximum price that a futures contract can move before trading is officially halted, and for some futures, trading will cease for the entire day.

For example, US T-Bonds have a daily limit of 3 points and if the market moves 3 points higher or lower from the previous day's close, no more trading is allowed above or below that level. If T-Bond futures closed last night at 104.5 the market cannot trade above 107.5 or below 101.5 today. You would, however, still be able to buy at the limit down price of 101.5 and sell at the limit up price of 107.5. The limits are there to try and reduce volatility and calm markets, but it is debatable whether they actually accomplish this goal.

Other markets such as the S&P500 or NASDAQ 100 stock indexes do not have maximum daily limits but have intraday trading halts. When implemented they force the market to close, usually for 15 minutes. As to where these levels are, they can change with the underlying volatility of the market, so make sure you check with your broker and understand the procedures behind them.

But don't get too concerned with limit moves because they rarely happen unless the markets are extremely volatile. Limit moves will occur in commodities such as soybeans during the growing season, limit moves on bonds happen during stock market crashes, etc. But although they happen irregularly you must understand them, and how they work.

HOMEWORK

This type of information is critical to the sort of homework that you must do before contemplating trading in futures. It may sound strange but many traders, when they first start dealing in these instruments never do the necessary research into the products they trade. Sometimes even the simplest information such as opening times, closing times, whether the market trades after hours, tick size, trading months, rollover dates, etc. passes them by. Make sure you approach the game properly and professionally and with due diligence and research.

YOU MUST HAVE A PLAN WHEN TRADING FUTURES

You must also employ some sort of trading plan with futures otherwise you will have problems, most likely a large and sudden move against your position. This coupled with the leverage involved can devastate anyone's account. Remember that if you lose 50 per cent of your capital you have to make 100 per cent just to get back to even, and as obvious as that statement is, many only realize it after it's too late.

But what sort of plan? This is up to you. You may base your trading decisions on charts, fundamentals, psychology or perhaps a combination of these. This is fine, but the most important part of your plan will be how you handle the risk factor. Make sure you use stops and stick to your plan when executing them as it's often said that in futures trading more money has been lost by traders not using stops, than all the other causes put together.

Another important part of your plan relating to risk must be to trade your account in such a way that everyday profits and losses don't mean much. For example, if your account is £50k then a daily P&L of under £1k will be easy to control without letting such demons as fear and greed enter your trading process. This is an important point; you really want to make sure that whatever happens in the markets you feel safe and comfortable with your trading, and it's highly unlikely that you will be able to do this if the account suffers from massive swings in either direction.

STUDY THE MARKET CHARACTERISTICS BEFORE YOU TRADE

The leverage available on a futures contract can be a beautiful thing, but it can quickly put you out of business if you don't respect it. Don't jump into a market unless you've looked back over time and studied its past characteristics. We strongly advise that you do this by looking at a chart covering at least the previous year or two to see how the market and price can behave. Be prepared when trading futures for unforeseen events and more importantly know exactly what you're going to do should they happen.

MULTIPLE CONTRACTS

When possible try and trade multiple contracts because this will give your trading more flexibility. Three or more contracts always works well because they will enable you to take profits and lock in gains on part of your position if and when the market moves in your favour. Or you can have the flexibility of starting to reduce risk as the market moves against you. If you trade just the one contract then it's very black or white, you are either in or out, and that often puts you and your trading at a disadvantage because flexibility is a powerful tool in anyone's toolbox. Trading more than one contract doesn't just spread your risk; psychologically it can be a benefit. All your contracts are unlikely to head south simultaneously whereas if you only have one on the boil and it bombs you will have nothing else to offer succour.

For example, you buy three Dow Jones March futures at 8,125 (each contract is worth $10 a point). As the market moves higher you lock in some profit by selling one contract at 8,225. The market continues to act well and you sell another contract at 8,350. With the final future you can now give the market plenty of room to move around, hoping for much higher prices. But if the Dow sells off then you've still taken some excellent profits by selling into the rally.

HOW TO USE FUTURES

Speculation

Pure speculation will be the main use of futures for readers of this book. In fact, it is often dryly noted that even the traders who state they're using futures for 'purely hedging purposes' are actually closet speculators. Futures don't have the best of images with many retail clients because they view them as far too risky. But futures themselves are not so dangerous if one trades them in reasonable size in relation to their trading capital. The traders who get into trouble are the ones that normally trade while undercapitalized or trade too large positions in relation to their account size. It wouldn't take someone with a £10k account trading five FTSE contracts long to either double their money or go broke. But what about the trader who has £100k trading the same sized position? In this situation they're only using leverage of around 2:1.

Don't make the mistake in thinking that futures are inherently risky and dangerous. The dangers can be effectively eliminated by knowledge, market understanding and a reasonably sized account in relation to the trades that are being taken.

Short-term speculation

If you use futures for short-term trading then you really must be following the markets at all times, especially in the fast moving and volatile stock indexes. If you attempt to trade part time then you'll always be at a disadvantage because you won't be able to react quickly to events, both good and bad. And swiftness is certainly a virtue to any short-term trader. Being quick to act may mean taking profits or dumping and reducing bad positions. But even if you can dedicate the necessary time, most people find that short-term trading is actually very hard. Think of how many 'day traders' there used to be in the stockmarket and ask yourself why they aren't still around? Day traders should be as comfortable going long the market as well as short so their disappearance shouldn't have much to do with the bear market since 2001. The reason has a lot to do with factors such as the cost of doing business, lack of discipline, not following a proper trading plan and the other common sense practices we encourage in this book.

But nothing is impossible and some traders do make a lot of money short-term trading, it's just that it is often not possible for the majority, including the authors. If traders do want to get involved in short-term trading futures then the best advice we can give is for them to realize that it may take the average person between one and two years before they feel that they have the necessary skill, patience and discipline to make a career out of it.

Medium/long term speculation

In our opinion better trading moves in most markets occur over the medium to long term (one week to a few months). This is also a more attractive time period for most people to trade in because you don't have to follow every tick from open to close. But you must get your time period right and realize that a lot of the daily moves are nothing more than what traders refer to as 'noise'. With 'noise' being the everyday slop and churn of prices.

But concentrating on the bigger picture without worrying about what happens today or tomorrow is easier said than done. Now we have the Internet, real-time prices straight to our desk, TV and other media constantly bombarding us with the latest news and views. It is therefore hard to resist the temptation not to metamorphose into a short-term trader. This is one of the aspects of why a disciplined trading approach is so important and must be worked on at all times.

To be a successful trader of medium-to-longer-term moves you must learn to be patient and wait for spots to place trades where the risk/reward ratio stacks up very favourably. You must also be selective in the trading signals that you take and be prepared not to participate in every move. Remember opportunities are made up faster than losses. Using charts is a good way to trade for the medium term, perhaps waiting for the market to move down to some sort of support zone before considering going long. Good traders will often wait many days if not weeks for certain patterns to set up, but the advantage of this type of trading is that you can follow a lot of different markets.

When you trade the medium-longer-term moves you must realize that your profits will be larger (than if short-term trading) but you will normally have to trade with larger stop losses. In order to counter the larger risk you must normally trade with smaller stops. A short-term trader in the FTSE may well trade an average of ten contracts; a longer-term trader may use an average position size of just two or three. Everyone wants to use the smallest stop losses possible when trading but don't think you can look for a 500 point move in the FTSE while risking only 10 points. Remember that good traders always try to set up their trades with a risk/reward of around 3:1, so risking 150 points to make 500 is an excellent trade, even if your chances of success are 50:50 over time.

Spread trading

Trading futures spreads is a common strategy for the professional trader, but only in contracts that offer multiple months to trade against, like commodities and interest rate futures. Spread trading is where you trade the price differential between the different months. In a futures contract like LIFFE's Short Sterling (three month interest rate) a trader may be expecting an imminent interest rate cut but no further easing in rates later on in the year. He would therefore buy the March contract while simultaneously selling the December. Spread trading makes up the majority of business in the interest rate futures markets.

Trading futures spreads is similar to how the 'pairs' trader operates in the CFD world (see Chapter 5 on CFDs for a full explanation). A spread is therefore not speculating on the overall direction of the underlying market, rather the price differential between the two contract months. So which is better, trading the outright or the differential? There's no obvious answer, but traders either tend to love spreads or loathe them. If you're good at simple arithmetic, and can quickly add/subtract in your head you may find that spread trading suits you. However, if you are like the authors and you always have to have a calculator handy, then our advice is to stick to trading the contracts outright. One final point on spread trading, you'll always be paying double commissions so make sure that you keep your costs down by dealing with a broker that offers very competitive rates.

Using futures to speculate on commodity prices

On paper one would think that high and low oil prices affect stocks such as BP and Shell, but this is often not the case as they buy and sell on long-term contracts that are not affected by the vagaries of the spot market on which the futures price is based. If you look at the correlation of BP's share price to the price of oil it's not that high, indicating that it is quite possible for the price of crude to go a lot higher while BP's share price goes lower. Therefore if you want to speculate on a commodity like oil, you're far better off trading the futures.

But commodity futures tend to have a habit of trading in a normal range bound or slightly trending market before suddenly exploding in volatility either up or down. This shouldn't come as a surprise because with a commodity you're dealing with a physical product subject to bad harvests, adverse weather patterns, or which can not be shipped quickly from one part of the globe to another. Remember most commodity futures are physically settled and therefore need to be delivered to warehouses, which may be on different continents to their country of production. A good example of how a commodity market can quickly change character is cocoa, which has been subjected to a massive squeeze pushing prices up over 200 per cent in little more than a year. Also note in Figure 7.1 the massive volatility from 2002 onwards. Get on the right side of one of these big commodity moves, and you'll never make as much money in such a short period of time.

But with the advent of financial futures the volume of commodity futures has drifted dramatically. Now the only people that use them are the trade houses and a few speculators left over from days past. Most new traders in futures look straight towards the fast-paced financials. Also a general multi-year bear market in commodities hasn't helped their volumes. But bear markets don't last forever so it is likely that during the next five years commodities will have their day again. If you're interested in trading futures always keep an eye on the longer-term commodity charts because no market offers traders the potential for such bumper profits.

Substitute tracker fund for the stockmarket

A stockmarket tracker fund is a fund that simply mimics the movement in an index. If the FTSE 100 is up 6.7 per cent over a year, a tracker fund will

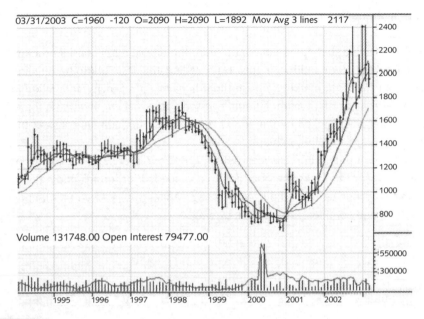

03/31/2003 C=1960 -120 O=2090 H=2090 L=1892 Mov Avg 3 lines 2117

Volume 131748.00 Open Interest 79477.00

Figure 7.1   Explosive bull market in cocoa

also be up around 6.7 per cent and vice versa on the downside. These are popular investment vehicles for many clients who get frustrated with fund managers talking a good game but never delivering. Transaction costs of buying into a tracker fund should also be relatively cheap, but with the greed of most asset management companies this is not always the case. Well capitalized investors have therefore started to create their own personal tracker funds by simply buying futures.

If the FTSE 100 future is priced at 4,000 then buying one contract would be the same as investing £40k in a tracker fund. Commissions will be drastically cheaper than buying into a commercial fund and managing the trade would be as simple as rolling the futures position over every quarter (a long position in the March contract is rolled in the June, etc.) And adventurous traders can also create a bearish tracker fund by going short futures.

→ summary

Like a good boy scout, 'be prepared' should be your motto when trading futures. Be prepared in your analysis including knowing the ins and outs of the product or products you're trading in. Be prepared for all eventualities of the trading day because with the leverage of futures, even mild moves against you can lead to large losses.

Traders who are starting out, in our opinion, should not really consider trading futures until they are confident in their own trading abilities. Stick to trading and investing in the stock market because there is plenty of volatility and action in that arena from which to learn. Futures and their potential will always be there, but don't get hoodwinked by the profits that are on offer, always consider the risks and damage that they can do.

If we haven't put you off the idea (which is not our intention – we just want you to be clear of the risks and discipline that is needed for futures trading) you can always 'paper trade' without committing capital until you are sufficiently competent, and confident, to start live trading.

8

Spread betting

COST FREE HAS ITS ADVANTAGES

For the uninitiated, spread betting conjures up a negative impression of gambling. They have the picture of men in flat caps or grubby raincoats with a cigarette stub clenched between their teeth poring over the *Racing Post* and surreptitiously slipping out to the high street betting shop for a quick flutter on the 3.10 at Newmarket. With that image 'sensible money' might turn its nose up at the idea of betting on financial markets. But it's funny how its ears prick up at the mention of 100 per cent tax-free gains. Just to repeat that for effect: spread betting profits are 100 per cent tax free. What is more, on UK shares there is no stamp duty and there are no commissions or charges whatsoever on any spread bet.

Spread betting is probably best known for the sport and novelty betting that allows punters to try their luck on big sporting events: bet the football, cricket, tennis, golf, American football or the Tour de France. For the sports betters there is the additional excitement and challenge that as the game or match proceeds the spread companies will continue to update and offer prices for clients to trade on. With a traditional high street bookie as soon as a football match starts no more bets are allowed. But spread betting (SB) firms are incredibly flexible and keep making a price right up to the end of the event.

The other types of bets that SB firms offer are so called 'novelty' bets such as the number of seats changing in a general election, whether O.J. Simpson was going to be found guilty or the winners and losers on TV shows such as *Big Brother*. Like financial spread betting any gains are tax free.

We think that the tax-free profits from spread betting are one of the best-kept secrets in the financial toolbox. To liken spread betting to gambling is to compare social drinking to alcoholism. Firms like City Index with professional offices in the City and pin-striped clients could not be further from the high street betting shop. With any sort of trading (and spread betting is certainly a form of trading) you can gamble as much or as little as you want. Spread betting is a tool that ranks alongside other sensible approaches to speculation and investment. Perhaps naming spread betting 'spreading' would instantly do away with the perception that it is gambling.

Spread betting is an exciting and innovative tool, but as with all forms of trading, whenever one is given an advantage it comes at a price. And the price of spread betting is that while your spread betting profits are tax free, your losses cannot be offset against tax.

HOW DO FINANCIAL SPREAD BETS WORK?

Spread betting companies offer markets in almost any available financial product as long as it has liquidity or is listed on a trading exchange such as London International Financial Futures Exchange (LIFFE) or the Chicago Mercantile Exchange (CME). Contracts on the big shares, FTSE 350, S&P500, EuroStoxx, bonds, currencies, commodities, stock indexes, etc. are readily available.

These bets may all sound very complicated but in reality if you understand what a bid and offer are, and what long and short means, you'll have no problem in understanding this industry, how it operates, and how you can effectively trade within it.

OPENING AND CLOSING A LONG POSITION

The first part that always confuses people about a spread bet is the difference between how traditional bookmakers and SB firms quote their prices (odds). High street bookies work with fixed odds like 10–1. If you place £10 at those odds (assuming no betting tax), and the bet wins, you'll pick up £100 plus the £10 stake. If you lose the bet, then £10 is your maximum loss. It's very simple.

But SB firms, whether on financial or sports bets, offer a two-way price. They never offer odds in the form of a fixed bet. With a two-way price many more possibilities are on offer, either you can bet that the price is too high or bet that it is too low.

If we take the FTSE 100 market as an example: SB firm makes a price of 4,100–4,106, or 4,100 bid, 4,106 offered. You feel that the FTSE 100 will rise significantly over the next few days and therefore you buy the spread at the offer price of 4,106.

But what are you actually buying and how much can you expect to win or lose should your trade go right or wrong? You're buying nothing more than an index, a number and therefore if the number/index goes up you'll make money and if it falls you'll lose. The normal minimum bet size is £1 a point. Therefore if you were to buy the SB quote on FTSE 100 at 4,106 at £1 a point and you sold when the bid price had risen 100 points to 4,206 your profit would be £100, with no tax to pay.

If the SB market on the index fell and you had the same bet or trade, what would your loss be? A spread bet is an open bet so to take your loss you have to sell out of it, or cover the trade. If you do not and the market continues to fall your losses will continue to mount. So if you bought the FTSE 100 index at 4,106 at £1 a point and the market moved lower you would perhaps take your loss by selling the index at say 4,050–4,056 (4,050 bid, 4,056 offered). As you would now be selling on the bid price your loss would be your initial purchase price of 4,106 minus the price that you 'covered' or sold the bet, 4,050 multiplied by your £1 stake. The loss in this case would be £56.

FURTHER DIFFERENCES BETWEEN SPREAD BETS & HIGH STREET BOOKMAKERS

In the example above where the punter placed £10 on the horse to win via a traditional bookmaker, he physically handed over the money. However, with SBs no initial money changes hands, all trading is done on margin. This is because a spread bet is an open-ended trade, while betting with Ladbrokes is a fixed bet. With SBs until you physically take your profit or loss in the actual marketplace, there is no way to actually quantify your net result. We go into more detail on this point later on in the chapter.

OPENING AND CLOSING A SHORT POSITION

SB firms offer a two-way price, so in order to go short, or profit from a down move in the underlying instrument you would be selling the market on the bid price.

If you are bearish towards British Telecom and the SB firm quotes you a price of £2.02–£2.04 you would open a short position by selling at £2.02 with an associated pound level per point. In this example let's sell short £5 a point of BT at £2.02.

BT's share price falls and we find that the SB firm is now quoting £1.74–£1.76. In order to take our profit we now have to cover the short position, or buy it back and so we purchase £5 a point at £1.76, the offer. Your profit is now £0.26 (or 26 points) multiplied by the original stake of £5 per point, making a total profit of £130.

Imagine this time that you had got BT's future direction wrong and the share price moved higher. The SB firm now quotes £2.19–£2.21. In order to take the loss you would again have to cover the short position and buy back £5 worth of BT at £2.21, the offer price. The loss on this trade would be £0.19 or 19 points multiplied by the £5 stake, a total loss of £95.

CLOSING POSITIONS

It is very important to understand that in either a long or a short bet your profit or loss will *never* be realized until you close or cover the initial bet. Spread betting creates a bet that must be 'managed'. Neither your ultimate profit nor loss will ever be known (unlike betting with a high street bookmaker) and it is unwise not to follow the performance of the underlying instrument or have some sort of stop loss employed (see below). Following the market's performance, of course, is relative to the timeframe you're trading in. If you were to buy the FTSE 100 index expecting a large move over the next few months, then following it closely on an intraday basis would in many ways be an uneconomical use of your time.

WHAT ABOUT THE SPREAD?

The spread or difference between the bid price and offer price will always be wider at a spread betting company than on the traditional product. For example, on the LIFFE market the bid–offer spread for the FTSE 100 futures is normally 1 point, while it is around 6 points on a spread bet market. Why is this so? This is the 'turn' for the spread betting company, and this is the price that the client pays for the advantages of spread betting: tax-free winnings, no stamp duty (on UK shares) and no commissions on *any* dealings. This means that even with the inherently larger spreads, dealing can be advantageous.

The spread betting companies are also dissimilar to the high street bookies in that they don't make money when their clients lose and vice versa. The spread betting company will in most cases immediately hedge off their risk in the underlying cash market. For example, if clients are buying a certain stock using spread bets, then the SB firm will buy the same stock (but in the cash market) as a hedge against his client's positions. The SB company's profit will therefore be just the spread that he charges for dealing.

ONE PRICE – THE CLIENT CANNOT TIGHTEN IT UP

If you wanted to buy Reuters' shares on the London Stock Exchange your stockbroker might quote you 212–214. You have the right if you want to tighten this spread up, perhaps placing a bid at 213 making the market now 213–214. But with SB firms you cannot tighten up their spread. So if they quote 211–215 for Reuters then that is the only price you can deal on, sell at 211 or buy at 215. You can, however, place bids below the market (to buy) and offers to sell above the market with the SB firms.

SPREAD PRICE VS CASH PRICE

In most circumstances the SB firms price will perfectly mimic the underlying cash price, plus their spread. Therefore if Vodafone was trading up 3.5p on the cash market the SB firms quote would also be up 3.5p. Some traders prefer, perhaps because they're trading off a chart to base their buying/selling decisions on the cash price. This can be easily done by informing the SB broker that your trades are to be executed off the cash levels. For example, you want to buy £5 a point of Marks & Spencers if the cash price goes to £2.10. By giving the broker this order he will trade for you on the prevailing spread quote if and when M&S goes to £2.10 on the London Stock Exchange.

When placing stop loss orders it is often a good idea to place your stops against the underlying cash price because there can then be no ambiguity as to whether you should have been stopped or not. With SB firms making their own prices and seeing all the levels of their customers' stops, clients have often argued wrongly that they shouldn't have been stopped out. This is normally the client clutching at straws; however, placing stop loss orders against a cash price negates any problems by letting the cash market be the judge and juror.

For example, you are long £5 a point of BT with the market at £2.00. You place a stop loss to sell the position at £1.75 against a cash price of £1.75 not the SB price. Make sure you understand this point as problems can often occur when it comes to stops being activated, especially in volatile markets.

WHAT ABOUT THE MONTHS?

Financial spread bets are quoted in different months similar to futures contracts. The normal months for financial products such as stocks, indices and bonds are March, June, September and December and the 'front month' is always the nearest month to the present date, assuming that it is not in the 'rollover' period. Therefore if you are trading in November the front month will be the December contract. If in doubt simply call your SB firm for guidance.

What is the 'rollover' period? This is when the front month rolls from say December into March, or to put it another way when the majority of the business moves from trading December to trading March. This normally occurs at a set date every expiry month and often differs from product to product. So you may find that fixed income spread bets such as gilts roll on a different date to UK stocks. Do not get bogged down on this type of theory, a quick call to your SB firm or a visit to their website will answer your questions.

Some spread bet contracts, notably on commodities, do not trade in the normal quarterly cycle listed above. It is therefore always wise to check what the front month is, when it rolls and what month it rolls into.

DIFFERENT MONTHS, DIFFERENT PRICES

First, with spread bets the price that you'll deal on will never be the same price as the product in the underlying cash market. If you're trading March FTSE the underlying FTSE 100 cash index may well be at 4,100 whereas the SB firm will be quoting 4,080–4,088. This price differential is known as the cost of carry and it is a mathematical equation that takes into account many factors such as interest rates and the reduced amount of money needed to control the asset due to the leverage. It is not worth worrying about for it will make you no money. Take the assumption that the professionals have priced the market correctly and concentrate on where the market is going, for this is where the money is made.

You will also see this price differential come into play with the different months trading, say, on the stocks. March Vodafone might be trading at 110–111 while June is quoted at 113–114. Does this mean that if you want to buy Vodafone for a long-term trade you'll make more money by trading the 'cheaper' March contract? No, because if you held the March till expiry and you wanted to roll the bet into June, the premium of a few pence would still be there. Always make the assumption with this kind of thinking that if there was any advantage one way or another then the professional traders would have got there first. Again don't waste time on the theory of pricing; focus on the future direction of the underlying.

HOW TO ROLLOVER A BET

You have a position in the December contract and the December is about to expire, with the March becoming front month. In order to keep the trade going you will have to rollover the position into March. You do this by simply instructing the SB firm to roll the trade forward. For example, you're long the December AstraZeneca (AZN) at £5 a point. By instructing the SB firm to roll it they would sell £5 worth of the December AZN and *simultaneously* buy £5 of the March AZN. Don't try to rollover the bet yourself because you'll end up selling the December on the current bid price and buying the March contract on the offer. During the roll the SB firms will quote a more beneficial price for their customers who want to roll bets.

What happens if you don't want to roll the bet over (or forget) and decide to let your December AZN expire? In this case the trade would be automatically settled against the SB firm's official settlement price, which is usually the Exchange's official settlement price plus/minus the spread. If you had bought the December AstraZeneca at £24.05 risking £1 a point and the SB firm's expiry price was £24.50, then your profit would be £45. If this is the case you now have no position in AstraZeneca.

This is important information to note because it is up to the client to rollover any bets that they have on, should they wish. If the SB firm doesn't hear from you before the expiry date then your trade or trades will automatically be settled at the expiry price. You cannot blame the SB firm if you didn't rollover, your bet expires and the market then makes a dramatic move in the direction you were anticipating the day following the expiry. Believe us, this happens a lot!

SPREAD BETS OFFER YOU FLEXIBILITY – MAKE SURE YOU USE IT

Use the flexibility on offer with all trading vehicles. Spread bets are a case in point. You do not just have to be in or out. For example, say you buy the FTSE 100 on a spread bet at £5 a point. If the market moves higher consider taking some profits. Remember, view your position as a percentage, and perhaps sell 25 per cent at a predetermined level, another 25 per cent at a higher level and then, maybe, squeeze maximum profit out of the remaining 50 per cent. A strategy like this actually works better on losses. Perhaps you entered into a short trade but the market's just not going lower or even edging slightly higher, peel off part of the bet as your original trading view is obviously not playing out but keep backing your original trading view with say a reduced 30 per cent trade.

Examples

A trader buys the March Vodafone priced at £1.00 at £10 a point. The market starts moving in his favour and when the SB bid price hits £1.05 he takes a profit on part of his position by selling £3.00; he is now long £7 a point. As the market moves even higher he decides to sell another £3 when the spread bet price hits £1.15 bid. The remainder of his bet (£4) he holds for any further upside potential.

Alternatively a trader may well have gone short FTSE 100 at £3 a point expecting a large fall during the day's session. He places the trade on the opening but by mid-morning the market has hardly moved, so he decides to lighten up by buying or covering £1 of his short position. Perhaps if the market moves higher or continues to trade in a flat direction he may well decide to cover another £1 of his short bet.

STOPS AND SPREAD BETS

Spread betting companies offer two types of stop losses, traditional stop losses that work in a similar way to those discussed in Chapter 4, and 'guaranteed stop losses'. The difference is simple; with a traditional stop loss you may suffer slippage if the market slices through your stop level. Slippage as you know is the difference between your stop loss level and the level you actually trade at. A guaranteed stop loss is what it says, it will guarantee that your stop will be activated at a certain price; there will never be any slippage.

Take Cable & Wireless as a good example. In early December 2002 C&W opened £0.28 down at £0.55 or 34 per cent lower. If you had bought the spread bet at £20 a point prior to this date and placed a normal stop loss to sell at £0.70, then this would have been activated right on the open, alongside every other seller in London, whether shares or spreadbets. Although £0.55 was the opening price it was likely that you wouldn't have been able to deal there, more likely around £0.50. Using a traditional stop loss you would have picked up about £0.20 of slippage or an extra £400 loss on a £20 per point bet. But if you had a guaranteed stop loss at £0.70 then this is the price that you would have sold at, even if the stock had opened at £0.10.

Why would anyone therefore not use the advantage of a guaranteed stop loss? Because the spread betting firm will charge you for the right, normally a percentage of the price. In the Cable & Wireless example the cost would have been around £0.02 or £20 × 2 = £40. Certainly a cheap price to pay in this example.

However, most professionals who use spread bets don't actually use guaranteed stop losses because they feel that their cost outweighs the benefit. Obviously the Cable & Wireless example was taken to the extreme. Professionals take the view that every now and then they'll get caught in a very adverse price movement, but the money that they'd save by not using guaranteed stops over a period of time pays for the odd disastrous event such as C&W.

Is there a right answer as to which stop loss to use? No, it's up to you but remember two points, first, the key factor with stop losses is that it is more important to have a stop loss than the exact level or method that you use. And second, always work out the cost of a guaranteed stop and ponder on a case-by-case example whether it is an economical use of your capital.

One final point with guaranteed stop losses, although they cost you money the SB firms will only charge you if and when the stop is activated. There is no charge for placing one of these orders or cancelling them. So use the flexibility that SB companies offer. Using a guaranteed stop loss may well be a sensible policy when, from time to time, you perhaps take on a monster position or you are trading a very volatile market. But with your normal trading you can stick to the 'cheaper' traditional stop losses.

MARGIN IS OFFERED

Trading on spread bets is always done on margin. If you were to buy £1 a point of Vodafone at 100p then theoretically the total value of that bet and the associated risk would be £100, if Vodafone goes bust. But to put up the maximum risk of £100 would defeat the purpose of spread betting. The SB firm will therefore charge you a deposit per bet that you trade. How much initial deposit normally depends on what is called the Notional Trading Requirement (NTR). How much of an NTR you will be charged per bet depends on the size of your stake per point, as well as the underlying volatility on the financial instrument. For example, a position taken out on British Telecom will require a higher NTR than on Tesco, because BT has the potential to move far more than Tesco whether on an intraday basis or from day to day.

The spread betting companies keep lists on what their NTRs are for every contract in which they offer a market. Traders that use their online software will instantly be able to see how much NTR is being applied for each position.

Some SB firms will also use what's called the 'Margin Factor' and this will be points that are multiplied by your original stake. For example, say the margin factor on the NASDAQ 100 index is 120, then in order to trade that contract at £2 a point (long or short) you would need at least £240 in your account, or have access to that amount on credit.

You may find that because of the added risks inherent in volatile markets or an event like 11 September 2001, that the spread betting companies increase their NTRs or margin factors across the board. If the margins are increased then the SB firm may well require you to reduce the sizes of your positions or deposit more money in your account in order to fund your current trades.

INITIAL AND VARIATION MARGIN

In all financial products that offer margin there are always two types of margin, initial and variation. Initial margin is the deposit that you must place in order to trade your account. In the above example of NASDAQ 100, the initial margin amount is £240. Initial margin normally stays at the same levels from product to product unless the markets get very volatile.

Variation margin is the amount of money that is credited and debited from your account on a daily basis as the market moves in your favour or against you. With all margined products, spread bets including all profits or losses for the day are deposited or withdrawn from the client's account. For example, you bought the FTSE 100 index at 4,100 risking £1 a point and the market closed 10 points better, your account would be credited the £10 profit even though the trade is still open. On the second day the market goes up another 20 points and therefore a further £20 would be credited to your account. The total credit to the account is now £30. But on the third day the market closed down 30 points returning to 4,100, the level that you initiated the trade. Your account is now debited £30. So although on the trade you have neither a profit nor loss, the daily profits and losses were credited/debited from your account on the variation margin basis. In fact, the software that all SB firms use is now so sophisticated that it will do this on a minute-by-minute basis.

MARKETS TO TRADE

The most common markets to trade with spread bets are those related to the stockmarket. Individual shares, stock indexes such as the FTSE 100, German DAX or the US NASDAQ 100. The SB firms will also make markets in most of the big European shares such as ABN Amro bank or Deutsche Telecom. Most of the shares within the broad US S&P 500 index are also available, alongside many technology shares. The SB firms are usually very accommodating and so if you ask them to make a market in a share they'll do their best to quote you a price, assuming that the client wants to trade a reasonable position.

Whatever product you trade always make sure you know the basic details such as opening/closing times, spread amount (difference between bid–offer), front month to trade, expiry dates, etc. You wouldn't believe how many people fall down at this hurdle.

CREDIT ACCOUNTS ARE OFFERED

Depending on your credit rating and liquid funds a spread betting company will let you open a credit account where no money needs to be deposited. The other alternative is to open a deposit account where usually a minimum of around £250 has to be used to set up the account.

Credit accounts can be a nice advantage but they must be used wisely. Trading on the financial markets is a very serious game where there is a lot of capital to be made by prudent and sensible decisions. The obverse is that if you view them as a casino then the likelihood that your money will quickly disappear is high. Personally we prefer deposit accounts to credit accounts because they give you the safety of only playing with hard money that you have in the account. Again, think potential risk over reward.

BROKERS

There are about a half dozen spread bet firms operating in London. We have consistently been impressed by City Index (www.cityindex.co.uk). They offer tight prices, and have excellent online software. Another big advantage that they have over their competitors is that you can download their software and trade a simulated account, risking no money while getting to grips with the business of spread betting. They also put on free introductory seminars around the country, and new traders to spread betting would be well advised to attend one of these if possible.

Spread bet firms like City Index have clients with a wide range of skills and knowledge. Don't think that just because you're new to the game, starting out or have a limited budget that they won't look after you, and make sure that you understand what you're doing. These companies are excellent at ensuring their clients understand what they are doing and how they can operate. One final point: spread betting firms are not allowed to give financial advice, as the client you must come up with your own ideas, but this is often good news as it will force you to do your own thinking rather than rely on some broker's opinion.

USES FOR SPREAD BETTING ACCOUNTS

The beginning trader

If you are new to the game of trading or want to test some ideas out in real-time markets then opening a spread betting account holds many advantages. The main one being that you can bet a fraction of the amount that you can on the Stock Exchange or futures markets.

We fully understand that many readers of this book may well be a little unsure of what they're doing and realize that experience with trading and markets is invaluable. The FTSE 100 future on the LIFFE market is priced at £10 a point and with moves of several hundred points in a day not uncommon, even a single contract can do a lot of damage to an account. But with a spread bet you can trade as low as £1. Make a major mistake for whatever reason and your losses will not get out of hand.

Spread bets are also an excellent way to get fully accustomed to the art and practice of short selling.

The hedger

Spread bets can be a very effective hedge for a stock portfolio. You may well have some money invested in stocks for the longer term, but feel that the FTSE could suffer some nasty falls in the future. To sell your stock, re-buy it alongside the actual cost of business, may well be prohibitive. Spread bets can be both a sensible and logical product to turn to. You could simply sell short the underlying FTSE 100 index or the individual shares that you hold, assuming they are not very small capitalization stocks as these are generally too illiquid for SBs to make a market. If your view turns out to be correct then you'd lose money on your stock holdings as the market moves lower but make profits via your short spread positions, and this profit would have the added bonus of being tax free.

If you were wrong in your bearish assessment and the market rallied then you'd make on your stock holdings but lose on your short positions, for a net result. However, in this case your losses would not be tax deductible. And if the market moved sideways then neither your stock holdings nor your short spread positions would be showing a profit or loss.

This is another opportunity to use and think about the flexibility to which we repeatedly refer in this book. Remember you don't have to be fully hedged: You might have £50k invested in cash stocks but only want to hedge part of this risk, say 25 per cent or 50 per cent. If the market did move lower you'd have some protection against losses to the cash portfolio but still enjoy upside potential if the stock market rallies.

The occasional punter

Everyday or every week speculation may not be your game, but every now and then a market takes your fancy, perhaps you feel that gold could well take off or that a busted-out stock may well be a good candidate for a quick rise. By using a spread bet you can easily and simply trade almost any type of view or scenario. You have the added advantage that most financial products can be traded within the one account. You first bet maybe in stocks, then currencies and then a US stock index, all easily done with spread bets and with a stake to suit anybody's pocket.

After hours trading

On the big stock indexes such as FTSE 100 and the American S&P 500 spread betting companies will make markets in so called 'after hours trading'. The London stock market closes at present at 4.30 pm but they will make a market in FTSE spread bets up until 9 pm. They'll also make a market before the stock exchange opens at 8 am. This adds yet more flexibility into a trader's arsenal. Not all markets are available for trading after hours so check with your spread betting company beforehand.

Different products – same markets

The SB firms are very inventive and often come up with new and interesting products to trade. You may find, for example, that if you want simply to go long the FTSE 100 index, they might offer you a few different types of spreads, perhaps a different quote for a daily bet (all trades automatically closed out at the close of business that day) or a monthly bet or perhaps some other type of market that they've engineered. This is an exciting and fast-paced trading world in which you need to keep yourself informed. Make sure you know what spreads your broker is offering, how they work and if there are any advantages or disadvantages in supporting your trading view. Also keep up to date on their websites and read any newsletters that they send you.

HOW TO MAKE MONEY WITH SPREAD BETS

The fundamental point you must realize with spread betting is the more trading you do, the higher your costs are going to be. And the more costs you have, the more they'll eat into your P&L account. In our opinion the best ways to use spread bets are either occasionally or for long-term moves.

Occasional use

Frequent traders of any product whether futures, stocks or spread bets should only trade if their cost of doing business is very low. This means not only low or zero commissions but also the ability to buy on the bid and sell on the offer. Obviously it isn't always possible to do this, but the ability must be there. Spread betting only fulfils one of these prerequisites, no commissions, but because with spread bets you will always have to pay the offers and sell the bids, the more trading one does the harder it is to make money, unless a very high percentage of your trades work out, which for most traders is unlikely.

The traders who use spread bets most successfully are often the ones that only trade when they have a good feeling about an imminent move, preferably a move with some real potential. Perhaps you see a chart pattern that says that the stock market has the potential to explode on the upside, this is a view that would suit a spread bet. But if everyday or several times a week you think that the market will rise a touch or fall a touch, trying to capitalise on these moves using spread bets is likely to result in a depreciation of your account

Long-term use

We have seen that the cost of doing business is a major factor in trading but in reality this becomes less of an issue if you trade occasionally. Therefore spread bets are excellent instruments for longer-term trading because the bid–offer spread becomes almost immaterial. If you buy the FTSE 100 index and make a gross profit of 40 points then the 6 ticks of bid–offer spread will be almost 15 per cent of the profit. But if you latch onto a move of several hundred points then this cost is not relevant. It's also not relevant if you lose several hundred points either.

A trader may well think that the price of crude oil is likely appreciate by $5 or more over the next few months. Spread bets are an excellent vehicle for these kinds of trades. Another trader may well be very bearish on the Dow Jones predicting a fall of over 1,000 points within the year; again spread bets are the perfect trading instrument for this kind of thinking. And with tax-free profits it makes these long-term trades even more attractive.

→ summary

Spread bets are actually very easy to comprehend. Understand what a long position is, what a short position is and how you both make and lose money respectively. Then determine if you want to go long or short, if long you'll always be buying at the offer price with a £ multiplier per point. Therefore for every point that the market goes above your entry price that will be profit times your monetary stake, and vice versa for losses if the market goes lower.

They are excellent tools for traders who want to become more experienced in different products or even learn the ins and outs of shorting the market. If you are thinking about opening an account then our advice is simple, take it slowly, make sure you understand how the trading works, bet small to start with and realize that although you may perfectly well understand the mechanics behind what you're doing there is no better teacher in trading than live market experience.

9

Information – you've got to sort it

THE INFORMATION AGE IS TRULY UPON US

Ten or fifteen years ago 'knowledge' about financial markets was confined to the golden circle who could afford a screen from Reuters or Dow Jones which gave them access to price feeds from stock exchanges and reliable financial news from around the world on a real-time basis. The reason it was confined to the elite was that the costs of the installations and their running costs were breathtaking.

The convergence of computers and telecommunications over the past few years has led to an information revolution from which you can benefit. With the advent of the Internet you can find information on almost any topic from an unbelievable range of sources. And 'unbelievable' is the watchword!

In other chapters we have inserted wealth warnings where there is a tool or strategy which we feel may not be suitable for the readers of this book. Information can be a blessing and a curse. Providers range from commercial organizations to the guy sitting at home publishing his own web page. Who do you believe? The fact that you pay for information is no guarantee of its value – ask the people who in one way or another paid for financial analysts' insightful assessment of Enron and WorldCom.

Prophets are never recognized in their own time. But do you have the time to sort the wheat from the chaff? How are you going to distinguish between the financial genius publishing a website or newsletter from his garret where he is starving for the cause of giving the financial markets the benefit of his wisdom and the charlatan ramping up some penny share he has sold to his mother?

Don't bother. One of the outcomes from this book (the authors hope) is that you feel sufficient confidence to make up your own mind about your financial future and how to manage it. Good newspapers will give both sides of the story and leave it to the intelligent reader to make up their own minds. Do you need to be led by the nose by some 'guru' or other self-appointed specialist?

The best investors take the raw data and make up their own minds. This book is not telling you to follow this trend, that fashion or the other fad. It is providing you with the tools for you to make what you will of the opportunities out there when you back your own judgement.

Having said that some paid websites and information sources are often excellent value either for the raw data like price feeds or to put issues on your agenda and in giving you the raw material to help you make up your mind about what strategy to adopt.

 ## TOO MUCH INFORMATION CAN DILUTE ITS USE

The trouble with the information age is that we are swamped by information and there is simply too much content and copy. A few years ago hard-pressed executives talked about 'information overload.' We have all had to assume that burden with the explosion of information sources.

Take any market or big stock like the Amazon.com or Vodafone and you'll find literally hundreds of research reports, views and analyses. Reading too much is counterproductive. It can lead to confusion; one report is bullish, another bearish, etc. It's also easy to make the mistake of only paying attention to information that supports your particular trading view. Good traders must always consider both sides of the argument.

 ## THE PRESS

The best way to sort the overcapacity problem is to find a small number of good sources while disregarding the rest. For example, with printed copy if you simply read the *Daily Telegraph* or *The Times*, the weekend's *Financial Times* and the *Investors Chronicle*, there would be little if any financial news that slipped through your information net. You would then have accomplished one major goal in the information process, keeping it simple and efficient.

While these publications are good for news and analysis there are a couple of warnings we would like to offer: first, newspapers take time to collect, print and distribute information. There are two dangers inherent in this. One is that the news is out of date by the time it reaches you. The other is that those who have access to instant, real-time news sources or are simply frequenters of the right City wine bars, will have known the story a long time before you rustle the pink pages over your cornflakes.

The second warning is that the views you will receive from the establishment press are the establishment views. The reason we felt it would be useful for investors if we wrote this book was because the mainstream press does not write about the tools and strategies that we discuss. Large sections of the financial services industry are unfamiliar with them or even spurn them – the press reflects this conventional view. The press is the messenger not the source: did the press warn investors about Equitable Life, endowments and Enron?

NEWSLETTERS

Then there is the 'anti-establishment press'. This is largely composed of the financial newsletter industry which often likes to see itself as contrary to or offering insights which have escaped the massed ranks of financial analysts and commentators in the rest of the press.

Be selective, there are some good, interesting, stimulating and amusing newsletters. Most of them offer a free trial and a free gift if you sign up. Part of the marketing is in the hope that you will not be bothered to cancel the direct debit. Our advice: try them out, be sceptical, drop those you do not think add value and remember to cancel the direct debit!

The messages and language that a lot of these newsletters use in their marketing material is designed to recruit subscribers who think they will 'get rich quick'. The tone of the newsletters is often breathlessly enthusiastic. When the stock market is in decline their marketing says 'buy into the next upwave', when the market is up they say 'sell before the crash'. Their track records seldom show them as being superior to conventional wisdom.

There is no evidence that the tips in newsletters are market beating. There is a danger in some of the newsletters that subscribers are invited to join 'exclusive' clubs, to be privy to the inner sanctum of some fictitious freemasonry which claims to be plugged directly into the movers and shakers of the world of finance.

THE INTERNET

The Internet adds a totally new dimension to the game. A lot of it is real time adding a great deal of urgency and immediacy to the information you find. There is a lot of it, a lot of it is free and a lot of it is rubbish. A major downside to the net is the sheer volume; you can literally spend all day, every day (and night) on it, bouncing from one site to the next.

The beauty of the web is that you are not constrained by the conventional view. There are great sites offering news and views, deeper explanations and insights into the tools in this book. Again the best strategy here is to find a few sites that fit your investing or trading niche, and stick with them. But from time to time bung your key investment words into a good search engine like www.google.com or www.metacrawler.com and see what's new. There has never been a time when so much that was new was available so quickly to so many.

Where to find the best information on the web?

The big financial sites such as www.ft.com, www.yahoo.co.uk (finance) and www.investorschronicle.co.uk are pretty good for company news and up-to-date market comments. If you need stock prices then these same sites carry delayed data which, for many traders, is perfectly good enough. Don't fool yourself that you need to pay an arm and a leg for real-time data – fifteen or twenty minutes delay is not going to make or break a well thought out trading strategy.

In our opinion most of the best financial sites are often the ones that are independently owned and operated. www.advfn.com and www.moneyam.com for UK stocks, and for US stocks, markets and economics www.siliconinvestor.com and www.financialsense.com are excellent.

Message boards

Message boards can be a great source of information especially for specialized subjects or stock sectors like technology, or futures-related markets such as commodities. The best message boards are without doubt the ones that are moderated to make sure that the good information and debate is not lost in petty 'flame wars' or bad language. If you find this kind of atmosphere on a board then chances are it won't add anything constructive to your trading. Also, look for boards that have rolling messages, rather than having to click on every heading, as this is a waste of time. Be careful when you first visit a site because a lot of the talk will be hot air. Even on the moderated sites people will normally be talking their own book, so be wary and cynical especially when it comes to tips.

However, that is not to diminish the value of these sites. You can find out all sorts of information and ask a lot of questions on these boards, A good example of a well run message board is www.gold-eagle.com which, as its name suggests, deals with ideas and views on the precious metals market. Here the only arguments you'll find are constructive ones. A message board like this can teach you all you need to know about a subject as long as you're patient and do not try to swallow what's discussed all at once. It is important to get a feel for what's being talked about and which message boards are worth listening to and which are not. This always takes time.

Another example of an excellent message board, but this time for education and trading ideas, is www.elitetrader.com . This is also moderated but this time for the simple reason of keeping spam adverts away. If a board is peppered with get rich quick adverts usually it has very little worth. For any traders with a naturally bearish view of the markets and world then you can't beat the US board www.capitalstool.com especially the hilarious 'mark to market' round up.

Can you use the message boards as a contrary indicator? That is, when everyone is too bullish, look to sell? Of course, this is always possible but remember the crowd is often right for a large part of any move and timing as ever plays the crucial role. What we advise is always to look for signs of extreme optimism, when board members are popping champagne corks or talking about buying new cars. If you see this kind of euphoria building it is often a good idea to lighten your position, tighten your stops or even consider going the other way.

THE INFORMATION 'LOOP'

Information is king so the saying goes, but only if you know how to use or interpret it. If access to information really was the trader's nirvana then the man in the street would have little chance of success in the markets against the financial powerhouses. But take a quick look at their financial record over the last eight years and these same powerhouses, like the

Grand Old Duke of York, seem to have ridden the bull market all the way up, and then all the way down. So much for their superior knowledge.

Don't fall into the trap of thinking you can't compete with the big boys because often the retail trader is at an advantage over the professional. Being an outsider allows you a greater degree of discretion in strategic thinking. What do we mean by 'strategic thinking'? In part it means being able to see the wood for the trees. The professional trader is often blind to opportunities arising from factors outside their immediate focus. It's ironic because many dealers on large trading floors with all the sources of information they could ask for complain that they would get better trading results without all the chatter, rumours and other tit bits of information floating around them all day. But then the investor sitting at home also feels that he would get better results if only he got access to the same information that the big boys. Having or not having information is often not the key, but how you interpret it.

INSIDER TRADING

Insider trading – company directors buying and selling shares because of privileged information they hold is a crime. It is a crime because it puts other investors at a disadvantage.

The purpose of the laws governing company information is to ensure that information reaches all participants simultaneously or as close to simultaneously as is practical. The theory is that the laws work for the smaller investor who is removed from the centre.

The way it works in the UK is that directors cannot buy and sell their own shares as they wish. They have access to confidential information such as forthcoming results and so are not allowed to deal in what is called the 'closed period'. Also, any deals they make outside this period must be reported to the Stock Exchange which in turn publishes them.

But is this information useful or does it burden the trader with yet more facts and figures? We would advise you not to get too excited about directors dealings unless they are selling, especially large percentages of their holdings. (See www.directorsdeals.co.uk and the weekend *Financial Times*.)

ANALYSTS AND STRATEGISTS

The financial world is filled with analysts and strategists but you must realize that in most cases they are paid to be bullish. How else can one explain why in the years 2000, 2001 and 2002 not one major house was forecasting a lower stockmarket? Surely that cannot be random. It will be interesting to see how their bullish forecasts do. Just look around you and see how much trouble recent cases on Wall Street regarding biased analysts have caused. The insider trading laws did not help investors in the United States who were victims of the incestuous link between investment banking and brokerage divisions of the same bank. A number of these Wall Street banks were fined $1.4 billion dollars for a range of practices which relied on inside information or a gilded 'circle'. During the 'high tech boom' those who gave the banks investment banking business were given the right to buy new issues that would be in high demand. At the same time brokers' analysts were restraining their views on firms with which their banking brethren had a profitable relationship. And investors were being well and truly shafted by brokers recommending stocks which in the privacy of their Wall Street offices they were admitting to each other were 'crap'. The cases basically reinforce their sole reason for existence, to bring in profit, whether fees from corporate deals or commissions from equity/debt broking and trading.

Should one therefore rely on the brokers and banks for financial advice? Ask yourself a simple question: from 2000 until today, do you think that a portfolio managed by a blindfolded monkey with a dart board tipping a shares in the FTSE 100 index would be in a worse financial state than a portfolio following the research of investment analysts? In our opinion it's very unlikely that the monkey would have done worse. And you may laugh at this suggestion until you find out that in a competition run recently in Germany, a monkey from the Berlin Zoo finished first in a share tipping contest!

Do your own research. Look around you, how do you see the economy, what's your view on interest rates, how is the firm that you work for or the industry that your friends work in doing? As long as you're logical, use some common sense and don't try to get too technical or too complicated in this arena; your information can be no worse than that of any analyst or strategist.

TRADING TIPS

On the whole listening to tips is pretty useless, with a profitable tip usually being offset by a losing one. The best advice that we've ever heard regarding tips comes from the excellent book *The Art of Speculation* by Philip L. Carret (J. Wiley) first published in 1930. Carret often mentions that having a cynical outlook to investment will save a trader many losses. On tips he goes on state that trader's should be humble when in possession of tips because rather than be the first to hear it, they're likely to be the thousandth!

Warren Buffet, the famous American investor, has also stated drolly that 'I love Wall Street because it's the only place I know where men driving Rolls Royces to work, get their stock tips from people taking the subway'.

Anyone who has spent an afternoon at the races is familiar with the 'hot tip' based on inside information. And like the races the markets are full of people who claim to have the inside track, inside information or the latest tip. But most, if not all, of this information is purely unsubstantiated rumour and is like believing that the hot tip in the 3.30 at Newmarket is really Shergar. But if you do want to act on tips or the like then it is always a good idea to trade only when you know that the tipster has also bought the stock or the product himself.

 ## PRICE FEEDS

Getting real-time information is only really necessary for short-term traders. If you're going to hold a stock for a few months then it is really not that important how it trades between 2 pm–3 pm on any given day. Many traders feel that with the fast-paced markets of today they need to be kept informed of all movements. But this can be very counterproductive and dangerous. If you are looking for a longer-term move and follow the intraday swings then it is easy to be panicked out of a position over the course of a 1–2 day reaction against your trade. Or even worse you get the impression that there's more money to be made by trading all the little moves. For example, if you buy a stock at £5.00 looking to sell it at £7.00 then in normal markets it may take a few weeks or months to reach this target. Perhaps it will go to £5.30, then trade back down to £5.10, power up to £5.80, back down to £5.45, etc. Successfully trading all of these moves may well give the nimble trader a profit potential of far more than the £2.00 that the long-term holder would generate. But even if you have the time to trade the moves, it is actually very hard for most traders and you may well find yourself paying for trying to be 'too clever'.

If you do need real-time prices then you have three distinct options.

1   A dedicated price terminal such as Bloomberg or Reuters.

2   An Internet price feed such as www.advfn.com for UK prices or www.prophet.net for both US and UK prices.

3   Your broker's trading software.

Choice 1 will likely set you back around $1,000 a month and you should only consider paying this if your yearly profits support the investment. Option 2 or 3 is normally best for 90 per cent of retail traders, but remember you will only get the best service if you have a fast Internet connection. If you haven't got one, we strongly recommend you sign up for a broadband or cable modem, not just for trading purposes but also for your research and general Internet work.

When it comes to your broker's online trading software be very wary about using it if it is browser based (runs through a web page). These are inherently slow and often indicate that the broker is well behind the times when it comes to offering its clients a good service. Always try and use a software package that is either Java based or where the actual program resides on your computer. Look at E*TRADE's online trading system for a good example of how it should be done (www.etrade.com).

LEVEL II DATA

Level II data is where you can see all the resting bids and offers above and below the current quote, and it is available either from your broker or as an add-on to whatever pricing service you're using. If the current quote on BT is 201–202, level II will show you all the bids and sizes at 200, 199, 198, etc. and all the offers above 202.

Is this information an advantage to the average trader? Most probably not for two reasons. First, everyone in the market is seeing the same information, so there is little or no edge to be gained. Second, and more importantly, level II data is full of 'spoofing' games. 'Spoofing' is where people try and give the illusion of bids or orders only to pull them should the market trade lower. For example, say a trader wants to sell a large number of shares and the current market is 502–504, he might place very large bids at 501, 500 and 499 to give the illusion that the share is well supported and to try and generate buy orders on his offer price. Then as soon as he's sold his shares he cancels his 'spoof' bids with a quick click of the mouse.

In order to use level II effectively you will have to gain a lot of experience and try hard not to get sucked into the perversity that is always present. Don't think otherwise and don't try and get too clever because the people you'll be battling against are likely to be hardened veterans of the level II trading world.

➜ summary

The information is out there, but as we've argued there's too much. Not only that, the markets seem to be obsessed these days with one or two days action. Just like a 'breaking' story on Sky News or CNBC, it only lasts as long as the next breaking, and normally unrelated, news event. The circus moves on very quickly. If you want to get good information then study sources, preferably independent, such as the net and newspapers until you discover who is worth listening to and who's not. This will always take time. Also, step back; don't get sucked into the whirlwind of news and price events that happen on a daily basis. Markets often move in ranges, effectively going nowhere from week to week before making a decisive move. These bigger moves are often where the good money is made and the news and context that fuels them normally builds up over a period of time.

10

Exchange Traded Funds

WELCOME TO 'SUPERSHARES'

Exchange Traded Funds (ETFs). Now there is a term to set the pulse racing! It is a bit like calling Champagne twice fermented grape juice or caviar dead sturgeon roe.

ETFs are probably the most exciting and potentially the most versatile instruments to have emerged in this generation of financial tools. According to one of the major players, Morgan Stanley, worldwide growth has been phenomenal: in 1993 there were three ETFs with assets under management of $811 million. In 2002 the number of funds had risen to 280 but the assets under management had risen to $141 billion. In the first month ETFs were listed in London (April 2000) the total value of transactions was £23.15 million. After peaking at £1.1 billion in July 2002 the value and volumes have contracted along with the rest of the market.

To keep up with how volumes are developing the London Stock Exchange has a useful site on these statistics: www.londonstock exchange.com/etfs/broker/performance.asp .

Paradoxically, while there has never been a more dramatic take-up of an investment instrument in recent times, ETFs are almost unknown among UK retail investors.

This could be because they have such a boring name. Or it could be that the firms sponsoring them either lack imagination or are fighting a rearguard action by the reactionaries from the unit trust and investment trust parts of their business which are set to crumble under the assault of these cheap (in commission terms) and transparent securities.

The sponsors are not devoid of imagination; they have invented brands like 'Spiders', 'iShares', 'Qubes', 'Vipers', 'streetTRACKS' and 'Diamonds' – which make up for the dull name bestowed on the instrument itself.

The first ETFs were listed on the Toronto Stock Exchange and called HIPS and TIPS. An early version called 'Supershares', created by a Professor Nils Hakansson in 1976, were wound up twenty years later largely because you had to be a professor to understand the prospectus.

But the value of the concept was not lost on the American Stock Exchange. AMEX was looking for ways to compete with its big brother the New York Stock Exchange. They took advantage of the fact that 'Supershares' been approved in a long and costly regulatory process at the Securities and Exchange Commission (SEC) and created Standard & Poor's Depository Receipts – 'Spiders' for short and ETFs were born.

Today the major world players in the world of ETFs are Morgan Stanley, Barclays Global Investors and Merrill Lynch. Barclays' iShares and Morgan Stanley's HOLDRS are listed on several exchanges: in the US on NASDAQ and AMEX and on the UK's London Stock Exchange (LSE).

It is perhaps surprising that stock exchanges like the LSE have not been more active in publicizing ETFs. Transactions for other collective investments like investment trusts are undertaken through the exchanges and the investment decisions taken by unit trust managers are executed through the exchanges as well. Purchases and sales of ETFs could lead to far greater volume and profit for the LSE and their members. This would be the case particularly if ETFs were to replace unit and investment trusts as the preferred collective investment vehicle.

 ## WHAT ARE EXCHANGE TRADED FUNDS?

Exchange Traded Funds (ETFs) are open-ended mutual funds, which trade as single shares, traded on stock exchanges that allow you to track the performance of a specified index or a sector:

- Domestic and international indexes such as the FTSE100, S&P 500 or NASDAQ.
- US, European and global sector funds such as basic materials, consumer cyclical and non-cyclical, energy, financial, healthcare, industrial, natural resources, technology, telecommunications and utilities.

Some examples of the funds available include:

- International for: Europe, Asia, the Americas and Global.
- By Market Capitalisation: Small cap, mid cap, large cap.
- By Value and Growth: Value and Growth funds.

An example is the iShares iFTSE100, which trades on the LSE. It tracks the FTSE100 Index, with shares trading at roughly 1/1000th of the index level. If the FTSE100 is at 4,000 the iFTSE share will be trading at around £4.00 per share. The performance of the share closely mirrors the performance of the index, including dividend payments, which go towards the payment of the total expense ratio of 0.4 per cent.

Another reason why ETF expenses are relatively low is because there is no shareholder record keeping. This is because the fund is tracking either indices or sectors and not being involved with the purchase of shares, which add considerably to the expense of running these funds.

ETFs offer the advantages of other collective investments like unit or investments trusts: they all allow investors to diversify investment risks across a number of shares or markets through one instrument. But ETFs deliver this advantage at a lower cost and with the convenience of an ordinary share transaction.

HOW ETFS WORK

The investor owns shares in a mutual fund that, in turn, owns the underlying shares in an index. The ETF shares issued to investors mirror the underlying portfolio of shares in the constituents of the index. That means that the capitalization of the ETF usually reflects the value of shares held in the index. 'Usually', because, although ETFs are issued in proportion to the shares in the index, the two will, from time to time, move out of line, particularly in volatile markets.

An example of an ETF – iShares FTSE100 Fund

- The fund consists of the 101 shares that make up the official FTSE100 Index and on 11 January 2002 the FTSE100 Index was 5,199.
- This example was taken from the iShare fund on 11 January 2002.
- The net asset value of one share on the 11 January 2002 was £520.22.
- The top ten shares in the portfolio, in order of weighting are shown in the table below.
- If you look carefully you will notice that there are five bank shares, two oil companies, two drug concerns and Vodafone. All of these shares in the table below account for 54.2 per cent of any move in the FTSE100 Index during trading hours

Name of Share	Share Price	Weighting %
1 BP	5.19	9.5
2 Vodafone	1.68	9.2
3 Glaxo	17.29	8.7
4 HSBC	7.90	6.0
5 AstraZ	31.15	4.4
6 RBOS	17.22	4.0
7 Shell	4.63	3.7
8 Lloyds	7.26	3.3
9 Barclays	22.86	3.1
10 HBOS	8.13	2.3

Source: iShares

 ## HOW THEY ARE PRICED?

Because they are quoted and can be bought and sold throughout the day the price will be determined by the value of the underlying shares the fund holds, just like a basket of real shares or your portfolio.

The price will reflect the movement of these shares and that is why you will not have wide discounts or premiums as you do with investment trusts. Behind the scenes market makers and computers monitor the price performance of the fund for arbitrage profits and the creation and redemption of ETF shares.

If ETFs were to trade at a premium over the net asset value (NAV) of the underlying shares the market makers would buy more of the underlying shares and sell more ETFs. If ETFs trade at a discount to the underlying shares the market makers would buy the ETFs and redeem them for the underlying shares which would be more valuable at that time. Some might say 'Nice business if you can get it'. However, it is not, as some literature says, a risk-free profit: market makers have certain privileges in the market for the risks they take in making markets.

 ## INVESTOR RISK

Given that ETFs are relatively new instruments to the UK markets it would be surprising if investors did not question the risks. The ownership of an ETF conveys title to ownership of a part of the fund, which owns the underlying shares. The risk is in the market and the value of those shares going up and down. The market makers, sponsors, advisors or managers can go bust but the trust will survive intact.

Although the investor is not the beneficial owner of the underlying shares, the benefit the investor has is of buying one security instead of all the underlying shares. Dividends are pooled and paid into the value of the fund and distributed in proportion to individual holdings less the appropriate proportion of the total expense ratio. This is not an important consideration, as ETFs have not been created as dividend paying instruments.

There is no leverage within an ETF. This means that the fund cannot borrow to increase its exposure to the marketplace. Accordingly, £100 invested will typically represent £100 value of equity exposure you are buying or selling.

Without wanting to sound like the marketing executives of an ETF firm we believe that, provided ETFs stick to their knitting – providing ungeared, transparent, low cost, easily executed, index- and sector-based investments – there is very little that can be said against them.

The real trick will be how investors use them within any proactive investment strategies they may have.

However, the ETFs may not exactly track the funds they are based on because of variations in fees, the fact that fees are deducted from daily net asset values means ETFs may underperform relative to expectations or against the benchmark index. Closing premiums and discounts on the calculation of the net asset value of the funds will affect reported performance; delays in dividend reinvestment can cause small underperformance in rising markets and small outperformance in falling markets.

Again this should not be a factor in not exploring and developing trading and investment strategies based around the growing demand for ETFs.

Our understanding of these (relatively new) instruments is that the underlying objective of the fund manager is as close a correlation as possible to the index he or she is following. 'Tracking errors' are temporary aberrations that appear to be an expectation of the funds' operations and are ironed out over short periods of time.

ETFS AND LEVERAGE AND DERIVATIVES

Split capital trusts became the financial scandal of 2002. It seems most investors, or perhaps their financial advisers, did not notice that the prospectuses allowed the split capital funds to borrow and buy units in each other's funds. There are no leveraged ETFs in the UK or for that matter in the US. ETFs that investors buy do not use leverage or derivatives like futures and options. However, in some marketing literature the market makers illustrate what they do to include transactions involving futures and options to offset the risks they assume. These are market-making transactions. The ETFs you, the retail investor buy do not use these instruments.

Recently, the concept of an 'actively managed ETF' in the US has attracted significant attention, even though many of the details regarding the potential operations of actively managed ETFs are apparently still in development. Unlike an index-based ETF, an actively managed ETF would not seek to track the return of a particular index by replicating or sampling index securities. Instead, an actively managed ETF's investment adviser could select securities consistent with the ETF's investment objectives and policies without reference to the composition of an index. We shall have to await events as the Securities and Exchange Commission is slow in making up its mind.

The purchase of an index-linked instrument such as an ETF is inherently safer than exposure to single stocks. Indexation also adds to the transparency in so far as fund managers are passive, following the index and not seeking strategies to outperform it.

That said ETF investors are targeting the performance of an index or sector and are therefore forgoing the opportunity to outperform it with their own investments.

 # TAX AND FUND EXPENSES

For tax purposes ETFs are not shares or securities as defined by Inland Revenue rules. They are investment funds and are treated as such for tax purposes. This means purchases are not liable for stamp duty at present. You will pay no tax on the income and capital gains if you invest in ETFs that are placed into Individual Savings Accounts (ISAs) or existing

Personal Equity Plans (PEPs). They can also be purchased for Self Invested Pension Plans (SIPPs).

An additional tax benefit is that because of the way in which the market makers undertake the transactions behind the scenes no 'tax event' occurs (the securities are in effect traded in kind not redeemed for cash) thus reducing the tax burden compared with other collective investments.

Morningstar, a US firm which independently monitors funds and fund performance shows that the average expense ratio of ETFs is considerably lower than for US mutual funds and this is the case with UK and European ETFs.

ETFs are bought and sold through your stockbroker or advisor and settled through Crest. This means that besides having real-time trading, which is not possible with unit trusts, the cost of ETF transactions is the broker's commission and the bid–offer spread, which can be at the same rates as other shares. There is no hocus-pocus in the total expense ratio as there can be with unit trusts where the unit trust investors are sometimes creamed by hidden charges.

As we have written about unit and investment trusts we thought it useful to point out the differences with the following box.

Unit trusts and open ended investment companies

Unit trusts and OEICs (open ended investment company) are pooled funds of investors' money, which are used to buy a range of shares, gilts, bonds or cash deposits. Both unit trusts and OEICs are open-ended funds meaning that the size of each fund can vary according to supply and demand. Unit trusts and OEICs provide a mechanism for investing in a broad selection of shares, thus reducing the risks of investing in individual shares.

When you invest in a unit trust you buy a unit, which means a portion of the total fund, OEICs issue shares. The fund manager will invest the money on behalf of the unit holders (or shareholders). The value of your investment will vary according to the total value of the fund, which is determined by the investments the fund manager makes with the fund's money. To cover the costs of running a fund you will usually have to pay an initial charge when units or shares are purchased, and an annual fee for ongoing costs such as administration. Some fees are declared as a percentage of your investment, others are built into the price.

▶

Investment trusts

An investment trust is a closed-ended collective investment fund. Investors' money is pooled together from the sale of a fixed number of shares a trust issues when it launches. The money is then used to buy stocks and shares in other companies to create an underlying portfolio of assets. The shares of a trust are traded on the Stock Exchange, meaning that supply and demand determines price and not the value of the underlying assets, although one influences the other. In most cases, a traditional investment trust has an unlimited life and issues one type of share known as an ordinary share.

WHEN IS AN INVESTMENT TRUST OR UNIT TRUST NOT AN . . . ?

. . . when it's an ETF. ETFs are a hybrid drawing on some of the best elements of more established investment instruments like unit trusts and investment trusts. But in the UK, because of lack of competition, there has been little incentive for the older structures to innovate. ETFs are set to change that and in the near future you can expect to see investment trusts and unit trusts changing to head off the upstart.

Table 10.1 shows the ways in which ETFs offer a more flexible and less costly vehicle for those who seek pooled investments to spread their risks.

 Table 10.1 Comparison with unit and investment trusts

	Unit trusts	Investment trusts	Exchange traded funds
Price vs NAV	3–5% spread	Discount or premium	None
Pricing	Historic	Diverges from underlying – discounts and premiums	Closely reflects underlying value of the portfolio
Charges & Fees	Initial fee of 5% and an annual charge of between 1% and 1.5% plus transactions costs (dealers fees and stamp duty)	Management fees and full expenses – review balance sheets for costs	Passive management fees are much lower than UTs or ITs. iSharesFTSE, for example, are only 0.35% per annum

Table 10.1 Continued

	Unit trusts	Investment trusts	Exchange traded funds
Listed	No	Yes	Yes
Transparency of holdings	Poor	Poor	Good
Independent managers	A unit trust manager can also be the distributor as well as sponsor	Not really	Can also be distributor or manager
Transaction	Via the manager – sponsor	Via your broker	Via your broker
Trading	Daily	Any time	Any time
Margin trading	No	Yes	Yes
Administration	In hands of the manager	Via management company	Fixed custodian fees
Processing and managers	Paper	Crest	Crest

ETF STRATEGY

So why use an ETF? To gain access to the world's investment markets in a risk-controlled and cost efficient manner, there are four headings to consider:

- **Accessibility** There is a wide range of funds to choose from.
- **Liquidity** With volume growing and the ease of trading, the pool of liquidity is as deep as or deeper than those of other collective investments.
- **Controlling Costs** Cost is an issue often overlooked by investors. With no stamp duty and low fees on ETFs it is up to you to find the best commission deals from a stockbroker.
- **Controlling Risk** If, for example, you invested in a sector ETF such as telecoms it would not be so painful if one company suffered a setback – it would not be a disaster.

ETFS – ADVANTAGES AS AN INVESTMENT TOOL

Being a passive, index-based investment, the managers of ETFs have no pride to injure if their portfolio is bruised by the vagaries of the market. This also keeps down the costs; the managers do not have to conduct allocation transactions except when the composition of an index changes. Also, they do not have to take the blame if your investment goes south – you chose which indices to track through your purchase of ETFs. And one of the beauties of ETFs is, of course, the wide choice you have of main indexes and indexes of sector funds.

The size of ETFs will in due course create huge liquidity and the facility with which they can be traded through a stockbroker ensures a far greater ease of transaction than for unit or investment trusts. Remember that unit trusts only have a daily dealing slot and as such are not suitable for trading nor do they disclose their portfolio positions.

ETFs are a WYSIWYG investment – what you see is what you get. ETFs only invest in the index they say they are investing in, so the investor always knows when he buys or sells exactly what is in the portfolio.

You have to have the resourcefulness of a detective to understand the charging structures of most UK collective investments. ETFs are much more transparent and cheaper. They are great building blocks for a portfolio. They can be bought in very small amounts and are attractive for pound cost averaging plans (PCA) (see page 203) in ISAs or SIPPS. But what makes ETFs particularly attractive is the way in which you can use them to manage your wealth. ETFs offer more choices of investment positions providing greater diversification. They are an ideal substitute for traditional sector funds. If, for example, you want greater exposure to a specific industry sector (such as property or banking), which you feel has greater potential than the broad market, you could add a sector fund in that industry to your portfolio. ETFs are an exciting innovation in allowing investors to diversify their portfolios using an instrument that is traded like a share and bears similar risks and costs. That makes them very attractive to large and small, experienced and inexperienced investors alike.

REGULAR SAVING AND POUND COST AVERAGING (PCA)

ETFs are attractive for regular saving and those who invest on the basis of pound cost averaging (PCA). PCA means automatically investing the same amount of money on a regular basis (usually monthly or quarterly), regardless of whether the price of the shares you are purchasing are high or low. It's a way to smooth out the market's ups and downs by averaging out your investment costs. Pound cost averaging gives you a number of advantages by eliminating the need to decide when to invest, helping you avoid the temptation of 'timing' the market and encouraging discipline in your investment strategies. The following example illustrates these points.

Example

Pound cost averaging using shares in X plc

Month	No averaging (one transaction)	Pound cost averaging
1	5,556 shares at £1.80 per share	1,111 shares at £1.80 per share
2	N/A	1,250 shares at £1.60 per share
3	N/A	1,379 shares at £1.45 per share
4	N/A	1,538 shares at £1.30 per share
5	N/A	1,667 shares at £1.20 per share

Total shares end value

The one share transaction	5,556	£4,630
Pound cost averaging	6,945	£8,334

In this example, both investment strategies lose money in the short term (remember, you each started with £10,000), but the 'pound cost averaging' lost less. This strategy had the advantage of cash sitting on the sidelines that did not lose value (or could even have been earning interest). And when the shares rebound, the PCA investor will be in better shape because they will always own more shares than you do. It is a sensible way to always get the average price over a period of time. What you must be careful about is the commissions you pay. Only deal at the most competitive rate you can find and if that means finding another broker then do so.

For the more experienced investor they have huge potential as a tool to manage their portfolios. Unfortunately many of these facilities are denied UK investors because British brokers lag behind their US counterparts.

PORTFOLIO MANAGEMENT AND DIVERSIFICATION

Asset allocation among equities, bonds and cash is the first step in the diversification of the risks inherent in any portfolio. Single stock risk such as that experienced by those who held Marconi shares or the employees of Enron who held their worldly wealth in Enron employee share options are examples of the risks diversification helps to minimize.

ETFs are ideal vehicles for diversification whether your whole portfolio is in a range of ETFs or if you have a mixed portfolio with a proportion of it devoted to collective investments. ETFs can be bought and sold if you wish to shift the emphasis of your portfolio periodically, by, say, rebalancing strategies and selling stock to crystallize gains. Recently introduced ETF bond funds add a further dimension to asset allocation and diversification.

SHORT SELLING

ETFs may be sold short, representing the sale of 'borrowed' shares in anticipation of lower prices when the borrowed shares must be replaced when the shares are repurchased. At present there are no UK brokers providing this valuable facility.

In the US ETFs are sold short to take advantage of overpriced sectors – sectors offer more choices of downtrends to short than do the broad market indexes – a clear price trend is the dream of any investor. This will keep investors from exposure to a single market trend. If there are 25 ETFs, given the ability to invest long or short, that gives investors 50 choices. You can go long on the strongest positive 'trend' sectors and short on the strongest negative 'trend' sectors.

ETFs also allow you to choose an uptrend from greater number of sectors in an apparently flat but, in reality, rolling bull market. You can make money in rising, falling and rotating markets. In short, you can do the portfolio management your traditional fund manager was supposed to do. You can also hold cash or neutralize your portfolio while your traditional fund will never do.

ETFs allow the investor to short the same sectors he is investing in long without realizing taxable gains by selling those sectors. Let us say you are faced with uncertainty in the market, such as that caused by the risk of war that hovered over the market for much of 2002 and into 2003. And let us say you are long in an index. You could switch 50 per cent of your holding to a short position in the same index. This would make your portfolio market neutral until the uncertainty passes. It is simply a way to preserve capital while still holding on to your core positions. The short offsets the long position and the portfolio's gains or losses are neutralized.

BUYING ON MARGIN

Buying on margin lets an investor borrow some of the money they need to buy shares in the hope of increasing the potential return on an investment. You do this by 'leveraging' your purchase by buying on margin. That may mean borrowing up to half of the purchase price from your broker. If you can sell the shares at a higher price than the original cost, you can then repay the loan, plus interest and commissions, and keep the profit.

However, if the shares drop in value, you still have to repay the loan. Despite its potential rewards, buying on margin can be risky. For example, the value of the shares you buy could drop so much that selling wouldn't raise enough to repay the loan. And, if you are forced sell the shares for less than you paid, your losses could be larger than if you had owned the shares outright because you might have held on in the hope of riding out the fall. Exchange Traded Funds may be purchased on margin, generally subject to the same terms that apply to ordinary shares. To buy on margin, you set up a margin account with a broker and transfer the required minimum in cash or shares to the account. Then you can borrow up to 50 per cent of a stock's price and buy with the combined funds. Let's look at the following example.

Example

- If you buy 1,000 shares at £10 a share, your total cost would be £10,000.
- But buying on margin, you put up £5,000 and borrow the remaining £5,000.
- If you sell when the share price rises to £15, you receive £15,000.
- You repay the £5,000 and keep the £10,000 balance (minus interest and commissions).
- That's almost a 100 per cent profit.
- Had you paid the full £10,000 with your own money, you would have made a 50 per cent profit, or £5,000.

Our model (Figure 10.1) explains how margin works when a share goes up or down and also keep in mind where your breakeven price is as well as building in a stop loss price for extra safety. Turn back to the Chapter 4 on stop losses to refresh your ideas on this valuable tool.

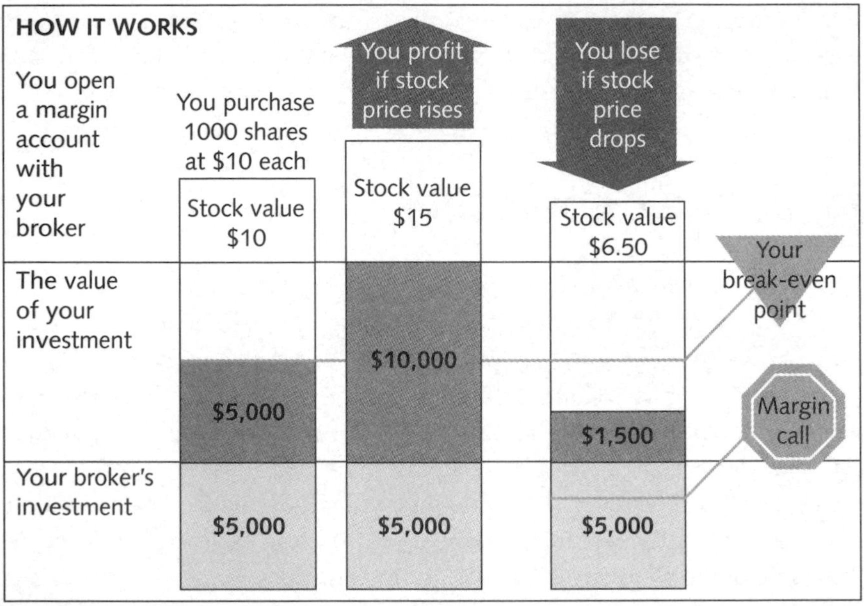

HOW IT WORKS

		You profit if stock price rises	You lose if stock price drops	
You open a margin account with your broker	You purchase 1000 shares at $10 each			
	Stock value $10	Stock value $15	Stock value $6.50	Your break-even point
The value of your investment	$5,000	$10,000		
			$1,500	Margin call
Your broker's investment	$5,000	$5,000	$5,000	

Figure 10.1 Buying on margin
Source: Morgan Stanley

Despite its potential rewards, buying on margin can be *risky*. For example, the value of the shares you buy could drop so much that selling them would not raise enough to repay the loan.

If the market value of your investment falls below its required minimum, your broker issues a margin call. You must either meet the call by adding money to your account to bring it up to the required minimum, or sell the shares, pay back your broker in full and take the loss. For example, if shares you bought for £10,000 declined to £2,000, the shares would now be worth only 20 per cent of their value at purchase. If your broker has a 30 per cent margin requirement, you would have to add £1,000 to bring your margin account up to £3,000 (30 per cent of £10,000).

KEY ELEMENTS OF EXCHANGE TRADED FUNDS

- ETFs can be used for many purposes by any type of investor. It could be your first investment for the long term, short term, benchmarking, hedging or speculation.
- They represent a portfolio of shares designed to track a specific index.
- They provide instant diversification and permit exposure to funds that either represent a broad-based market index, a specific industry sector or an international sector.
- There is no stamp duty.
- They can be traded throughout the day with 15-second price movements.
- You can hedge your complete portfolio by selling short.
- You can margin your purchase and sales of ETFs.
- No sales loads, although you still pay your stockbrokers commissions.
- Clearing and settlement of ETFs is just like any other share.
- Dividends accumulate and are paid out at regular intervals.
- Management fees are deducted directly from the dividend yield and are less than other collective investments.

→ summary

Expect to read more about ETFs in the financial pages of the newspapers and financial magazines over the coming years. We predict they will become one of the most popular tools for retail investors and that they will give unit trusts and investment trusts a run for their money. We may even find some collective investment funds transforming themselves into ETFs.

ETFs can take a good deal of the hassle out of a commitment to the equity markets; you don't have to spend your time researching individual stocks and can concentrate on other financial planning issues like diversification and tax.

The reason for our enthusiasm for ETFs is simple: they are easy to understand, they are easy to trade, the costs are low. They allow the investor to diversify their risks easily and reduce costs effectively; not only are the costs low but the ability of even a novice investor to build a well diversified portfolio means avoiding the need to pay a financial adviser for something you can do yourself.

They are also flexible tools that you can use to enhance your returns or hedge your position by shorting or buying on the margin.

In *The Investor's Toolbox* we have concentrated on equity-based tools. A truly balanced portfolio will have a proportion of fixed income investments. The bond-based ETFs, which are now coming to the market will be a further tool investors can use to diversify their risks and build a balanced portfolio.

11

Hedge funds

'THE JONES THAT NOBODY CAN KEEP UP WITH'

Alfred Winslow Jones was a Harvard graduate and he travelled the world as a purser on a tramp steamer before becoming a journalist in Spain during the Civil War and then a diplomat in Nazi Germany. After the Second World War he contributed articles to *Fortune Magazine* on the current fashions in investing and market forecasting. In doing so he came to the conclusion that he had a better system for managing money than the so-called experts. In 1949, he raised $60,000 and using $40,000 of his own money began putting his theories to practice in a 'general investment partnership', which became the first hedge fund.

The innovative principle behind Jones' investment approach was 'hedging'; he balanced his long share positions by selling short other shares to protect against market risk. So, the term hedge fund was born. Hedging is essentially a 'safe' investment strategy. The dictionary defines hedging as 'avoiding making a decision or giving a clear answer' even 'being evasive or shifty' and invokes the use of 'hedging one's bets' where one will back both sides so as to avoid betting losses or loss of face in an argument. A pure hedge fund is theoretically an investment that will go nowhere but will protect the investor against the vagaries of the market.

But Jones took the concept a step further evolving it into the hedge fund vehicle with which we are familiar today. It is the funds that use leverage (borrowed money) and short selling like those run by George Soros (Quantum Fund) and Julian Robertson (Tiger Fund) to enhance the potential return on the partnership's assets that have hit the headlines in recent years. They have been accused of everything from breaking the Bank of England to destabilizing South East Asian economies, hyperbole which the managers did not dismiss to protect a 'macho markets' image. They have been even more reticent when they have racked up huge losses, which demonstrate the risk of these types of leveraged funds.

Jones called short selling and leverage 'speculative tools used for conservative purposes'. In 1952, he transformed his general partnership into a limited partnership and introduced another wrinkle, an incentive fee for himself as managing partner amounting to 20 per cent of the profits. His entire liquid net worth remained in the partnership. This one man was responsible for combining short selling, leverage, incentive fees and shared risk–the four most common characteristics of the classic hedge fund into one investment vehicle. And quite a package it turned out to be. Operating in almost absolute obscurity for seventeen years, Jones' success was finally brought to the public eye in a 1966 *Fortune Magazine* article titled 'The Jones That Nobody Can Keep Up With'. In addition to uncovering his unique investment strategy, the article revealed that his partnership had outperformed the best performing mutual fund that year by 44 per cent and the best five-year performing mutual fund at the time by 85 per cent, net of all fees. This article attracted the attention of both wealthy individuals seeking better investment returns and talented professional investors willing to sacrifice big salaries for profit participation in the portfolios they managed. By 1968, there were approximately 200 hedge funds.

The Dark Ages

Unfortunately, many of the new hedge fund managers weren't really hedging at all. Shorting even a small percentage of a portfolio restrained performance in the go-go markets of the mid–late 1960s. So most hedge fund managers simply stopped doing it. They were leveraged long – a particularly risky business in less liquid and non-accommodating markets. This produced some big hedge fund losses in 1969–1970 and major bloodletting in the savage 1973–1974 bear market. The more prudent hedge fund operators survived, but many most closed the doors.

The term 'hedge fund' became a misnomer from the time Jones started using short selling and leverage. As well as having nothing to do with neatly trimmed privet hedges dividing suburban gardens, most of the products available today do not have as their objective the hedging of a portfolio. They are most likely to engage in leverage and short selling and the purchase of other financial tools to enhance the return of their investors' money. However, it might still be said of them that they 'hedge out' their exposure to the market.

The Renaissance

The hedge fund industry limped along until the early 1990s, when the financial press once again began trumpeting the returns achieved by hedge fund superstars George Soros and Julian Robertson. Many hedge funds no longer resembled the classic long/short equities model developed by Jones. For example, Soros made his big killing in the currency markets and Robertson employed modern financial derivatives such as futures and options, which didn't exist when Jones started his fund. With lots of new hedging tools and a tide of favourable publicity, the hedge fund business exploded.

Two of the legacies that these funds retained from Jones were that the investors in theses funds mostly required the promoters to have a large chunk of their own wealth in the funds as Jones did. The Americans picturesquely refer to this as 'eating their own cookie'. The promoters still also take 20 per cent of the profits for their trouble – but of course share substantially in the losses if they are eating their own indigestible cookie.

The Enlightenment

A further spur to the creation of hedge funds has been the growth of increasingly oppressive regulation as lumbering regulators and unimaginative institutional investors struggled to keep up with the creativity and innovation of investment managers. The frustrated managers packed their bags and headed off to less restrictive climates to form exciting investment vehicles for the clients they took with them. Unsurprisingly they called these investments hedge funds. Most of their clients were 'high-net-worth-individuals' (known to the rest of us a 'the rich', a term presumably too vulgar to use in hedge fund marketing literature). The hedge fund industry is founded on and thrives on innovation. Yet to an extent parts of it have come full circle. Hedge funds evolved into a number of broad categories in which investment mangers specialized in particular strategies.

A HEDGE FUND STYLE GUIDE

As is the case with UK investment and unit trusts or US mutual funds, many different styles of hedge funds are available. Each hedge fund style tends to define a unique profile in terms of expected risks and investment strategies, as summarized in Table 11.1. However, hedge funds may switch styles frequently, depending on the individual fund manager's judgement. This is another aspect to consider and monitor.

Table 11.1

The style	The strategy	Expected risk
Market neutral	Long and short positions weighted equally; focus on share picking	Low risk
Convertible arbitrage	Goes long on convertible securities and short on underlying equities	Low risk
Opportunistic	Trading oriented	Low/moderate risk
Growth	Targets actual growth and growth potential in earnings and revenues	Moderate risk
Value	Shares are chosen based on assets, cash flows and book values	Moderate risk
Quantitative	Focuses on computer-driven analysis	Moderate risk
Distressed securities	Buys the shares of companies in reorganization or bankruptcy	Medium Risk
Macro	Focuses on shifts in the global economy	High risk
International	International shares are purchased	High risk
Leveraged bonds	Leverage applied to bonds and fixed-income derivatives	High risk
Emerging markets	Shares are purchased in emerging financial markets	Very high risk
Short only	Short positions are taken on individual securities	Very high risk
		Very high risk

Source: Alternative Investment Management Association

Hedging, in the sense of a balanced, short/long portfolio was a distant memory until the emergence of a the concept of different sector funds being brought together into one holding in what became 'funds of funds'. These 'funds of funds' allowed investors to spread risks among the various hedge funds offering different investment strategies. A further turn of the circle is that in seeking better returns for their investor's institutional funds like pension funds are now investing a proportion of their money with hedge funds. So your pension fund company has probably placed a few per cent of your pension with a range of hedge fund managers in an attempt to squeeze a bit more return than can be achieved from 'plain vanilla' stocks and bonds.

Frequently, as a result of the investment freedom they have created for themselves, hedge funds may have different correlations with traditional investments, such as bonds or major market indices like the FTSE100 or the American S&P 500 Index. This in itself represents a form of hedging, an offsetting of the risks inherent in the main body of a portfolio.

WHY INVEST IN HEDGE FUNDS?

You may say to yourself: 'these are fancy funds for rich people located in remote jurisdictions with a light regulatory touch. What can they possibly have to do with me and my investment goals?'

No one 'bets the farm' on any, single investment vehicle. Similarly a hedge fund is a tool to help fine-tune your investment strategy: one that can be used as a substitute for some of the strategies we recommend or as part of your investment approach. In being a substitute you can take advantage, through a single fund, a range of funds or a fund of funds, of the capacity to:

- actively manage investments;
- leverage;
- short sell;
- hold derivatives positions;
- hold cross-holding; and, oh yes
- hedge!

WHAT ARE THE RISKS OF INVESTING IN HEDGE FUNDS?

1 Unregistered funds

Single hedge funds of funds generally invest in several private hedge funds that may not be subject to UK registration and disclosure requirements. Many of the normal investor protections that are common to most traditional registered investments are absent. This makes it difficult for investors to assess the performance of the underlying hedge funds or independently verify information that is reported. All of this can make it easier for an unscrupulous hedge fund manager to engage in fraud or mis-report to their shareholders. (See Regulation and due diligence below.)

2   Risky investment strategies?

Hedge funds often use speculative investment and trading strategies. Many hedge funds are honestly and well managed, and balance a high risk of capital loss with a high potential for capital growth. The risks hedge funds incur, however, can potentially wipe out your entire investment. If you can't afford to lose your entire investment then perhaps you should see hedge funds and funds of hedge funds as a spectator sport.

But if you decide you do want to be a participant you should always ask the following questions before investing:

- Is there a daily or regular calculation of the funds net asset value (NAV)?
- Does the management make it clear what market strategies are used, how they will be used and the risk to reward ratios for the shareholders?
- How often will investors be sent fund reports? Remember how fast markets can move in the electronic times we live in.
- Can the performance of the fund be followed on the Internet?

3   Lack of liquidity

Hedge funds, both the unregistered and registered variety, are basically illiquid investments and can be subject to restrictions on transferability and resale. Unlike investment and unit trusts, there are no specific rules on hedge fund pricing. Registered hedge fund units may not be redeemable at the investor's option and there is probably no secondary market for the sale of the hedge fund shares. In other words, you may not be able to get the money you invested in the hedge fund back when you want out of the investment. Hedge funds investments are not for 'rainy day money', you need to be in the position to decide when to withdraw the investment and not have that decision forced on you by your circumstances.

You must always check with the funds prospectus or with the managers what the redemption policy is as well as making sure that it conforms to your investment risk profile.

4 Regulation and due diligence

Hedge funds are coming home. The Financial Services Authority (FSA) is allowing investment banks to offer hedge funds to the wider public and the investment funds are packaging these funds in 'bite sized chunks', which allow them to be incorporated in Individual Savings Accounts (ISAs). The sponsors and managers of these investments have done a rotten job in marketing them: they have not made them any more attractive for those selling them than selling basic investments like cash ISAs and they have failed to educate financial advisers and the public. Potential investors still seemed confused by all the financial jargon used by the managers and the performance for UK funds has been very disappointing compared with their battle hardened US counterparts.

Many offshore hedge funds are just unregulated pools of money from wealthy investors, operated in a secretive manner with little or no regulatory or other accountability. As more hedge funds are created, the more they will look toward individual investors to be their next source of funding. That is one reason why there may be concerns between UK and US regulators and industry watchers that the proliferation may lead to scams.

Most ordinary investors do not have the time and resources to undertake the due diligence that is required to establish the credentials of offshore funds. The new breed of hedge funds that are accessible to the UK investor are mostly regulated and this insures the investor against fraud to a limited degree. These funds will publish prospectuses and will mostly be managed by large and recognized institutions. However, that in itself is no guarantee of performance.

5 UK Tax Consequences

Hedge funds will normally be deemed to be 'trading' and not 'investing'. If there is a UK investment manager, it is important to ensure that the UK 'investment manager exemption' is available otherwise the fund may be subject to UK tax on its trading profits generated through the investment manager. The Inland Revenue is always on the lookout for new tax revenues and we caution investors to bear this aspect of due diligence in mind.

The vast majority of hedge funds are non-distributing funds and UK residents as individual investors will be taxed income tax (rather than capital gains tax) on any dividends and gains on redemption.

All this may change under a recent Inland Revenue consultation aimed at reforming the tax treatment of all offshore funds. Investors in 'non-qualifying funds' (including most hedge funds) would be required to calculate their share of taxable income from the fund on an annual basis whether or not that income is distributed.

MANAGER'S SKILLS

It has been said that the only priceless ingredient in a hedge fund is its management. Investor success results entirely from picking the right managers. It is not a strict asset-allocation decision. Hedge funds involve all existing asset classes, including stocks and bonds, and are all about investment strategies. In this way, hedge funds are unlike investment trusts, which obtain most of their returns from the stock market. Most of the returns for hedge funds derive from strategies followed by an individual manager. After all, the whole purpose of a hedge fund is to hedge out exposure to the market.

The investment is in the fund manager, in his strategies and in his ability to generate a return in different market environments. Any investor who is contemplating investing into the hedge fund market now has a wonderful chance to look at all the manager's performance results. Anyone who has beaten the benchmarks during the 2000–2003 bear markets deserves to be considered.

Perhaps more than with other forms of investment you need to investigate the manager of the hedge funds in which you may be interested in investing. The leading hedge fund research company is called Allenbridge Hedgeinfo – part of the Allenbridge Group plc. They compile in-depth reports for institutions and their wealthy clients, which look at all the significant criteria we have mentioned in this chapter (see Useful addresses and websites on p. 243).

The prospectus will give you the background of the manager and there are also websites and news stories in specialist publications that go into detail about managers' backgrounds. Heed them; while past performance in investments is not a guide to the future profitability of an investment, a manager's pedigree counts for a great deal in the hedge fund arena.

FEES

Basic management fees for hedge funds usually hover around a basic 1 per cent, but the important figure is the performance fee that will spirit up to 20 per cent of the profits into the manager's personal pocket. But as you can see from the net returns shown in Table 11.2 you are still better off in most hedge funds than in most investment and unit trusts even after the performance fee has been deducted. Our research shows that, historically, most funds have earned sufficient returns to justify those fees. Like anywhere else, diversification is essential. The best way to invest in hedge funds is through a fund-of-funds product that includes at least five (perhaps as many as ten) different hedge funds within a portfolio. But here again you must choose a manager who is going to do the picking of the managers of the funds, which make up the whole portfolio. He has to be very proactive and all the parties must have some of their wealth tied up in the funds and *not* the management company.

Over time you are likely to develop a comfort zone with hedge funds. A lot of rich people have been investing in hedge funds for a long time. Most still are. Those who understand them, and invest accordingly, find they are a useful additional means of diversification in a well-structured portfolio. However, research is the key: you need to keep a very close eye on all movements of the management, portfolio and advisers, especially in the UK where the industry is still young and inexperienced when compared with that run by battle-hardened American managers.

Table 11.2 Comparative performance of hedge funds

Style/strategy	Net compound annual return	Standard deviation	Van ratio	Sharpe ratio
Van US Hedge Fund index	17.0%	9.1%	3.0%	1.6
Van Offshore Hedge Fund index	14.4%	9.3%	6.1%	1.3
MSCI World Equity	4.3%	16.2%	39.4%	0.2
S&P 500	11.1%	15.5%	23.8%	0.7
Morningstar Average Equity Mutual Fund	8.2%	15.9%	30.3%	0.5
Lehman Brothers Aggregate Bond index	8.7%	4.5%	2.6%	1.5

Source: Van Hedge Fund Advisors International, Inc. and/or its licensors, Nashville, TN, USA

COMPARING MUTUAL AND HEDGE FUNDS

In addition to the average hedge fund outperforming the average mutual fund, the highest returning hedge funds significantly outperformed the highest returning mutual funds, as shown in Table 11.3.

Table 11.3   **Five-year net compound annual returns, 1st Q/97 to 3rd Q/02**

	Hedge funds	Mutual funds
Top 10	31.8%	16.1%
Top 10%	24.6%	6.2%
Top 25%	19.0%	3.7%
Bottom 25%	–4.5%	–9.1%
Bottom 10%	–12.4%	–12.3%
Bottom 10	–22.1%	–28.6%

Source: Van Hedge Fund Advisors International, Inc. and/or its licensors, Nashville, TN, USA

Looking to the Allenbridge Group for some guidance in how they recommend UK and European hedge funds we find that they take into account all the aspects we have mentioned in this chapter. They look very carefully at performance and management skills, as well as the structure of the fund and how well the fund matches their objectives. Over the months they will watch how the managers are performing and report to their client base.

From all their experience they created the following rating scale:

- A, A–   91–100 per cent superior quality
- B+, B, B–   61–90 per cent satisfactory
- C+, C–   51–60 per cent weak to doubtful
- D and NR   0–50 per cent not satisfactory, not rated, no information

➡ summary

So should you have hedge funds in your portfolio?

Traditional money managers base their careers on the assumption that their ability to pick good shares or bonds can add value. Adding value for a traditional manager means picking shares that generate a rate of return high enough to cover the fees they charge, while netting the investor a little extra return on top of popular stock indexes. While the merits of traditional managers are in perpetual debate, hedge fund managers would argue that they have a much greater potential to add value.

Bearing this in mind here are some rules to follow:

- Hedge funds are unique and can offer good upside potential. However, despite their glamour and recent mainstream acceptance, they're risky and success will depend to a large degree on your research into the manager.
- Most hedging strategies have much less stock market exposure than most traditional investment and unit trusts. Many individual UK funds will not be worthy of your investment capital so any hedge fund exposure might best be achieved through a fund-of-funds approach or even looking at US funds but add to your considerations the currency risk of exposure to a US investment.
- Hedge fund allocation is best defined as a percentage of an investor's equity weighting. A maximum of 20 per cent or so of an investor's equity weighting is a reasonable rule of thumb. So, if your portfolio mix is 50/50 in shares/fixed income, etc. then you should put no more than 10 per cent into hedge funds.
- Hedge funds are crossing the threshold from wealthy investors and Institutional Investors' tools to retail product. Whereas boutique hedge funds rarely attract the attention of the financial media, the likes of JP Morgan, Citigroup, HSBC, Deutsche Bank have all helped to raise awareness of hedge funds generally. And therein lies the problem: hedge funds are not subject to general media analysis. Once again careful research is required.
- So hedge funds are not what they say they are, i.e. hedged investments; many of them are highly leveraged or highly speculative. However, if it is pure hedging you are after you may be able to create your own hedge fund using the techniques and tools we have described in this book.

12

Covered warrants

AN ARRAY OF WARRANTS

So what's new? Haven't covered warrants been about for years? Well, yes and no. Ordinary, plain vanilla warrants (we'll come to the covered ones in a moment) have not only been about for years but have been accessible to the retail investor. These warrants are the ones listed on the stock exchange and issued by companies (including investment trusts) that are themselves listed.

Investment trusts issue call warrants, which have a separate quote. The warrants give you the right, but not the obligation, to buy shares at a fixed price on a fixed future date. You can buy them just as you do shares, through your broker. By buying them you are securing the right to buy shares, which will have risen above their face value when the fixed date arrives. Or, if the expectation is not fulfilled and the warrants do not change in price or indeed fall in price, they expire on the due date and what you paid for them is lost. All you are buying is a right. Benefiting from the right is contingent on the underlying shares being worth more on the expiry date than they were when you bought them.

However, the essential element is the leverage you gain. You lay out a small amount now (keeping your capital safe or earning money elsewhere) in the hope or judgement that the underlying shares will rise above the price at which you have the right to buy them. In this way you buy the shares 'cheap' when you exercise the right at the expiry of the warrant. Alternatively you sell the warrants for a profit prior to or on the exercise date and make a profit. Or you exercise the warrants to buy the shares and sell them there and then for a profit.

All this assumes that the underlying shares have risen. If they haven't your outlay on the warrants dies on the agreed date, you have lost your outlay – but that is the full extent of your loss and the risk to which you were exposed.

UNCOVERING AND DISCOVERING COVERED WARRANTS

Now we come to covered warrants. And yes, they have also been about for years. But in the 'Johnny-come-lately-nanny state' that is modern Britain our guardians and protectors felt we were not mature enough for these 'dangerously radical' instruments.

Like unlicensed drinking hours our Continental cousins have enjoyed trading and dealing in covered warrants for a long time. Germany has about 24,000, Italy some 6,000 and even Australia has had a thriving market for many years.

The British investor is now considered mature enough to imbibe this financial cocktail. From 28 October 2002 a number of institutions signed up to the Stock Exchange's Central Warrants Trading Service. Since October 2002 the number of covered warrant trades has grown from around 700 to just over 2,500 in May 2003, with a combined monthly value of some 6 million.

But far from rushing to the pub like an eighteen-year old to quench years of alcoholic deprivation the British investor has sauntered down to the hostelry and merely sipped at what in terms of financial risk is more the equivalent of a ginger beer rather than a shot of moonshine.

Covered warrants begin life as naked as babies. A covered warrant is a proprietary instrument, issued by a financial institution such as Goldman Sachs, a bank, that bestows on the holder the right, but not the obligation, to buy or sell an asset at a specified strike price during, or at the end of, a specified time period.

The first issuers also include JP Morgan Chase, Soc. Gen. and Unicredito, trading as TradingLabs. Two others, Commerzbank and Dresdner Kleinwort Wasserstein, may issue warrants with a listing on the LSE but with trading taking place away from the order book.

These sponsors issue the warrants on shares, baskets of shares or indexes. They thus sell the right (but not the obligation) to a buyer of the warrant to acquire the underlying share, basket of shares or index for a fixed price on a fixed date. The term 'covered' means that when the sponsor, such as Goldman Sachs, sells a warrant contract to an investor the sponsor will 'cover' or 'hedge' its exposure by buying or selling the contracts underlying shares in the stock market.

COMPARING WARRANTS AND OPTIONS

Warrants and options are born out of shares, bonds, indices and a few other products. Like warrants, options also have a lifespan, an expiration date and an exercise price, and their prices depend on the same factors and develop in the same way as warrant prices.

Options have their own market and in the UK this is Euronext/LIFFE. Brokers on behalf of investors on the London Stock Exchange. Option contracts are standardized, which means that most are issued backed with rules regarding their lifetime, size and price. Warrants, on the other hand, can be issued on many different types of underlying values, whereas the option market focuses on domestic shares, indices and bonds. Table 12.1 on page 228 explains some of the differences.

CALL OR PUT?

The holder of a covered warrant has the right but not the obligation to either buy (call) or sell (put) an underlying asset at a predetermined price known as the exercise price on or before a certain date in the future. A call warrant rises in value when the underlying asset rises in value, while a put warrant rises in value when the underlying asset falls in value.

You would buy a call warrant to take advantage of a rise in the price of a share you wanted to own or simply to profit from the increase in the value of the warrant. You might buy a put warrant in the hope that the value of the underlying shares will fall but that you will receive the price agreed at the outset of the contract. They can be stock settled or settled for cash, where the holder takes the difference in cash. Holders of covered warrants tend to settle for cash to avoid the payment of stamp duty.

The cost of owning the covered warrant's right is the premium one pays and if you take into consideration that this premium is a fraction of the value of the underlying asset, this is the maximum amount of money the holder can lose.

AMERICAN OR EUROPEAN?

Covered call and put warrants can either be European or American style. A European style warrant allows you to exercise your right only on the expiry date, whereas with an American style warrant you can do this at any time between the listing date and the expiry date. Covered warrants traded in the UK are invariably American style.

Table 12.1 shows some of the differences between three different instruments, all of which have been covered in different chapters of this book.

Table 12.1   Differences between covered warrants, traded options and CFDs

	Covered warrants	Traded options	CFDs
Securitized derivative	Yes	No	No
Continuous trading during market hours	Yes	Yes	Yes
Paperless settlement	Yes	Yes	Yes
Stamp duty (if cash settled)	No	No	No
Included in ISAs	No	No	No
Wide range of underlying (may include global coverage of equities, indices, baskets, commodities)	Yes	(Depends on contracts set by LIFFE)	Yes
Always hold a long position	Yes	No	No
Buy a short position	Yes	Yes	Yes
Limited and quantifiable loss	Yes	Depends (if writer or buyer)	Depends (have to use stop-loss)

Source: London Stock Exchange

USING COVERED WARRANTS

Covered warrants have some of the key advantages of a derivative tool: they can be used to profit from falling as well as rising markets, their gearing can be used to help improve returns or they can be used to protect portfolios against adverse market movements. Finally, the risk of covered warrants is limited to the amount invested. The benefit of the limited liability concept again.

GEARING

By committing to a covered warrant premium the investor is gaining control over the value of the underlying security, which is a multiple of that premium.

Gearing in simple terms means you are going to have to put up a lot less of your capital rather than buying shares outright for cash. This can produce two different equations and the example, shown in Table 12.2 needs to be studied carefully.

Table 12.2

	XYZ plc call Warrant	XYZ plc Share price
30 June 02	300p	£32.00
14 August 02	430p	£33.90
Profit	130p	190p
Per cent return	**43.33%**	**5.94%**

In this example the value of the covered warrant has increased by 43 per cent for a 5.9 per cent change in the underlying share price (430p–300p). It is also important to remember that gearing works in both directions, so a fall in the share price will also cause a greater percentage fall in the value of the covered warrant.

A similar chart in Figure 12.1 gives the differences between a Put and Call covered warrant.

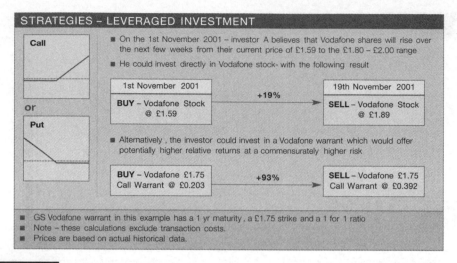

STRATEGIES – LEVERAGED INVESTMENT

Figure 12.1   *Source:* Goldman Sachs (2002)

HEDGING

Covered warrants provide you with the opportunity to manage your risks by hedging. They allow you to take a view on the market, to go long or short, to insure yourself against market movements, which will reduce the value of your portfolio.

Covered warrants are sold as puts and calls respectively, the right to sell or the right to buy an underlying security. Thus if you consider a market or a particular stock likely to rise in price you would buy a call giving you the right to buy the underlying security at a given price and at a given future date.

Conversely, if you anticipate a market or share will fall you could sell a put allowing you to sell the underlying instrument at a price and on a date that you agree at the time of your purchase of the covered warrant. So if you believe that the oil sector is due to take a 'knocking' you might buy a put on BP or Shell. Figure 12.2 gives a good example of hedging a portfolio or a position.

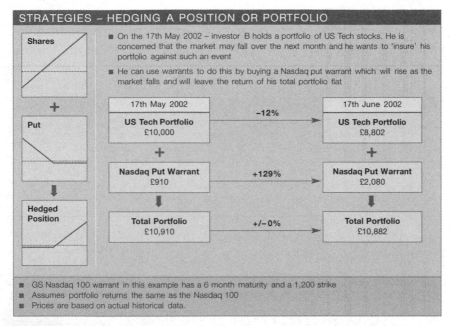

Figure 12.2   *Source*: Goldman Sachs (2002)

 FREE YOUR CAPITAL

If in your plans for allocating your money to shares or indexes you buy covered warrants instead of the underlying securities you have the identical upside exposure as you would forking out the full amount for the underlying instruments. That means you can take the cash and put it somewhere else such as a no-load money fund, you could simply bank it for interest (not that you would earn much in today's low base rate environment) or buy some other investment.

Look at Figure 12.3 to see what we mean by extracting capital from all or parts of a share portfolio.

The joy of being an investor or Name in the Lloyds of London insurance market a few years ago was that you did not have to put up any money 'up front'. You agreed to insure a risk but could use your capital to earn money elsewhere until a plane crashed or hurricane swept through the Caribbean or whatever. It was when claims for the victims of asbestosis had to be settled that the myth of this particular free lunch was exposed and many Names ruined. The moral here is always to keep cash available and in a secure investment.

Covered warrants do not carry a downside market risk. You pay the premium and if the market goes against your view you lose the premium. When you insure your house and it does not burn down you lose the premium.

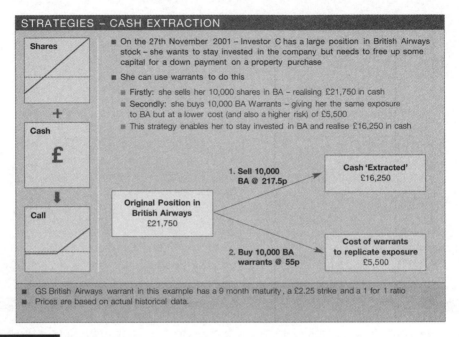

STRATEGIES – CASH EXTRACTION

Shares

+

Cash

£

↓

Call

- On the 27th November 2001 – Investor C has a large position in British Airways stock – she wants to stay invested in the company but needs to free up some capital for a down payment on a property purchase
- She can use warrants to do this
  - Firstly: she sells her 10,000 shares in BA – realising £21,750 in cash
  - Secondly: she buys 10,000 BA Warrants – giving her the same exposure to BA but at a lower cost (and also a higher risk) of £5,500
  - This strategy enables her to stay invested in BA and realise £16,250 in cash

1. Sell 10,000 BA @ 217.5p

Cash 'Extracted' £16,250

Original Position in British Airways £21,750

2. Buy 10,000 BA warrants @ 55p

Cost of warrants to replicate exposure £5,500

- GS British Airways warrant in this example has a 9 month maturity, a £2.25 strike and a 1 for 1 ratio
- Prices are based on actual historical data.

Figure 12.3   *Source*: Goldman Sachs (2002)

PORTFOLIO DIVERSIFICATION

An important part of any risk management programme is diversification of your investments across assets (shares, bonds, cash) but also within sectors and across sectors and markets. Covered warrants are issued on individual stocks like Vodafone, and sectors like retailers and markets, which allow you to diversify your share ownership without buying the underlying product.

Substitute for derivative products

The longer expiry terms, small size, market making and the clearly contained risk mean covered warrants are easier for individual investors to manage than other derivative products like futures and traded options.

Liquidity

Liquidity in little traded covered warrants can cause problems. But in actively traded covered warrants there is liquidity similar to that in major shares.

 TAX

Since most covered warrants are cash settled with the investor receiving the profit in cash rather than exercising and taking the underlying asset no buy or sell trade has taken place on the underlying security. This means, under current tax law, that there is no stamp duty on the contract note.

Covered warrants may be held in a Self Invested Personal Pension (SIPP) with any tax advantages that may hold, such as exemption from CGT on profits though there is no allowance for offsetting losses. However, they cannot be held in an ISA and they are subject to capital gains tax above the annual exemption limit of £7,500 when you buy and sell them in your own name.

 ADVANTAGES OF COVERED WARRANTS

Unlimited Potential

If you have bought call warrants in a bull market or put warrants in a bear market the theoretical profit potential of warrants is unlimited.

Gearing

Some see the strong market reactions of covered warrants to the changes in value of the underlying security as a risk.

Pre-determined Downside

The premium you pay for your covered warrant is a fraction of the price of the underlying security. However, you gain control of a much larger investment with the downside limited to the premium paid.

Long or short expiry dates

Covered warrants normally have a life of six to twelve months but can extend for up to three years. This means that the value of newly issued warrants is less sensitive to time decay and grants greater flexibility than other derivatives.

Small minimum sizes

The minimum amount necessary to invest in covered warrants is relatively small and is within the reach of most investors. However, we must warn our readers to check all their dealing costs before entering into any small contract commitment.

HOW DO YOU BUY COVERED WARRANTS?

Covered warrants are bought through your broker in the same way as ordinary shares. They are subject to new commission tariffs and are settled through Crest. Unlike traded options there is no minimum contract size and no restriction on the range of stocks, commodities, indices and currencies that can be dealt.

Some brokers are charging what is called a 'round trip' commission of £50: that means £25 to buy or sell and the same again to close the trade. Based on an average trade of below £5,000 this seems expensive even though the broker may argue that they offer a telephone service and research. We urge all readers once again to pay close attention to what can be called the 'cost of doing business'.

PRICING ELEMENTS OF COVERED WARRANTS

- Current share price.
- Time to expiry.
- Level of interest rates.
- Exercise price.
- Dividend paid on the underlying stocks (which the warrant holder does not receive).
- Volatility of the underlying share.

The price of a covered warrant is principally based on the price of the underlying share or index. The volatility of the underlying will be transmitted to the covered warrant. However changes in the price of the warrant arising from changes in the price of the underlying share are not linear. A rise or fall in the price of the warrant will not be constant in relation to a unit variation in the price of the underlying share.

The result is that the warrant price breaks down into two components: the intrinsic value and time value.

In Figure 12.4 all the component parts of pricing a covered warrant are shown. You will have read in Chapter 6 (Traded Options) how these parts all fit in and work.

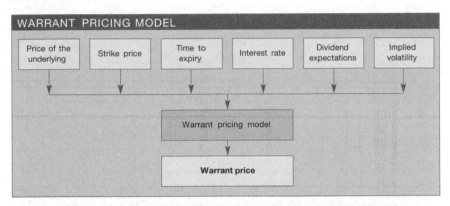

Figure 12.4 *Source*: Goldman Sachs (2002)

Intrinsic value

The intrinsic value of a call warrant is the amount by which the price of the underlying asset exceeds the exercise price of the warrant and vice versa for a put warrant. You arrive at the intrinsic value by deducting the strike price from the current value. If the current value exceeds the strike price the covered warrant is 'in-the-money', if the strike price exceeds the price of the underlying share the covered warrant is 'out-of-the money'.

For example, you buy a Vodafone call warrant that entitles you to buy Vodafone shares at a strike price of 100p in September 2004. With the shares trading at 96p the call warrant would be priced at, say, 21p, which would be 4p out-of-the-money without any intrinsic value. If by the end of March 2005 the stock moves up to 125p the warrants would be priced at 35p and have an intrinsic value of, say, 25p. The remaining 10p is the 'time value' and decreases in value the closer the warrant comes to expiry. Note the leverage that the covered warrant offers: the share price has moved up 30 per cent, while the warrant price has risen 75 per cent.

Time value

The time value is the premium on the intrinsic value that the holder of a warrant is prepared to pay in the hope of making higher future gains. The size of this component depends on a number of market factors, such as:

- Interest rates.
- The residual life of the warrant.
- The expected yield associated with the underlying.
- The expected volatility of the future price of the underlying.

Time value can be calculated as the difference between the market price of the warrant and its intrinsic value. The market value of at-the-money warrants and out-of-the-money warrants coincides with time value. Time value is highest when the warrant is at-the-money.

Figure 12.5 explains the various parts we have explained above and in the Traded Options chapter.

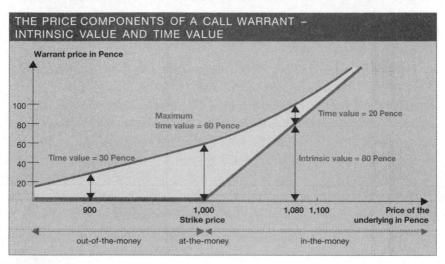

EXAMPLE – TIME VALUE

A call warrant has a strike price of 1,000 Pence.
The conversion ratio is 1:1 and the
price of the underlying is 1,080 Pence.

Intrinsic value:	80 Pence
Time value:	20 Pence
Price of the warrant:	100 Pence

THE PRICE COMPONENTS OF A CALL WARRANT –
INTRINSIC VALUE AND TIME VALUE

Warrant price in Pence

Maximum
time value = 60 Pence

Time value = 20 Pence

Time value = 30 Pence

Intrinsic value = 80 Pence

| 900 | 1,000 | 1,080 1,100 | Price of the |
| | Strike price | | underlying in Pence |

out-of-the-money · at-the-money · in-the-money

Figure 12.5 *Source*: Goldman Sachs (2002)

→ summary

- Covered warrants are comparative newcomers to the London market although they have been tried and tested in other markets for a long time. In Germany, for example, they have been very popular with retail investors. Education has to be developed to kick-start this new market.
- Many of the features of covered warrants echo the market in traded options: they are a right but not an obligation; the right to buy is a call, the right to sell is a put.
- The LSE listing regulations have set rules where covered warrants will have maturities of between three months and three years. A useful addition when trying to make a judgement over market events, the price of shares and how this will help your investment strategy.
- Like traded options they are attractive tools for the retail investor as they can be used for speculation, hedging, portfolio diversification and allow for the freeing up of capital as they are geared vehicles allowing the investor to put

up a small sum to control a much larger investment. They also have the advantage that provided they are not exercised they are free of stamp duty.

- The advantage they have over traded options is that they can be traded through your normal broker, you do not have to find a specialist options broker.
- Covered warrants are a very flexible tool and the issuers have the capacity quickly to create new vehicles to allow opportunities to react to new market trends or demands.
- However, before investing, it is a good idea to keep in mind what your strategy is – the reasons why you are going to trade, the time period and the risk and reward you are entering into. One excellent site you should use is www.gs-warrants.co.uk and log onto the Scenario Selector. Once you have entered all the data the selector will calculate the various returns that each of the warrants will generate under your scenario – excluding taxation and broker's fees. The calculations take into account the erosion of time value, value and volatility and the bid–offer spread you pay as an investor.
- On the same site you may want to analyze an individual warrant such as Vodafone. Carefully load up all the data into the system, as this tool will prove useful as you seek to select a warrant that matches your investment view.
- Consider using our stop loss principle (see Chapter 4) and remember it can remove the emotional side of investing and save you a great deal of your capital. However, you will need to look after this side of your investment strategy, as most brokers are not equipped to help you.

Appendix: Comparing the tools

If you are new to some of the tools in *The New Financial Toolbox* this table will demonstrate the differences and the similarities in their use:

	Covered warrants	Traded options	CFDs	Spread betting	ETFs
Continuous trading during market hours	Yes	Yes	Yes	Yes	Yes
Stamp duty	No	No	No	No	No
With ISAs	No	No	No	No	No
Wide range of equities/indices	Yes	Yes	Yes	Yes	Yes
Long trades	Yes	Yes	Yes	Yes	Yes
Short trades	Yes	Yes	Yes	Yes	Yes
Quantifiable losses	Yes	See below	Stop loss	Stop loss	Stop loss
Expiry of positions	3 months to 2 years+	3 to 9 months	Open ended	3 monthly rollover	Open ended
Commissions	See below	From £1.70 to £20 per deal	See below	Nil	See below

- **Wide range of equities and indices**
  All five tools offer traders the choice of shares to go long/short or use as hedges and gamble on a wide range of indices.
- **Quantifiable losses**
  The only tools where you can predict a quantifiable loss is with covered warrants. All the others require discipline as to when to close a position or in the case of CFDs, spread betting and ETFs the correct use of the stop losses, which is why finding a stockbroker who offers a stop loss facility is so important.
- **Expiry of positions**
  This is a tricky one as you can see there are from 3 to 9 months for traded options but covered warrants can go up to 2 years with the rest as open positions depending on your investment strategies.

- **Commissions**

  We have spoken about the cost of doing business in each of the chapters relating to the tools and in the above chart we examine some of the parameters you should look at carefully. The website www.broker-advice.com offers an excellent free service on finding the correct broker at the right commission for many different products.

- **Covered warrants**

  We feel that some of the 'round trip' commission charges are far too expensive. We have mentioned £50 round trips and with the average contract size of £5,000 this is a very expensive commission to pay. Please refer to www.broker-advice.com .

- **Traded options**

  London brokers' charges range from £1.70 per contract to £20. Yet again we ask traders the check the cost of doing business as well as checking sites offering up-to-date prices for comparison before trading.

- **CFDs**

  Because of the gearing effects all brokers will want a margin of at least 20 per cent of the cost of the transaction. Go back to Chapter 5 to remind yourself about how this type of deal is structured.

- **Spread betting**

  See what we wrote in Chapter 8 about the structure of the bet. It looks as though you are not paying a charge but the profit for the bookmaker is in the spread or bid–offer price you see on the screen. Check out websites to compare prices and open an account at every financial bookmaker if that is your way of trading.

- **ETFs**

  As they trade just like shares your broker should be charging you his standard rates. However, we feel that if you are trading or managing your own proactive portfolio then only trade with brokers who offer the most competitive prices both online and offline.

Useful addresses and websites

Financial bookmakers

City Index Ltd
Freepost LON21292
London
EC2B 2BB
Tel: 020 7550 8500
www.cityindex.co.uk

Covered warrant and option sponsors

Goldman Sachs International
Peterborough Court
133 Fleet Street
London EC4A 2BB
Tel: 0845 609 1555
www.gs-warrants.co.uk

CFDs brokers

E*TRADE Securities Ltd
42nd Floor, One Canada Square
Canary Wharf
London E14 5AA
Tel: 0845 045 6060
www.etrade.co.uk

Hedge fund advisers

Allenbridge Hedgeinfo
Allenbridge Group plc
30 Hill Street
London W1J 5NZ
Tel: 020 7409 1111
Fax: 020 7629 7026
www.hedgeinfo.com

Exchange traded fund sponsors and advisers

Morgan Stanley Investment Management
25 Cabot Square
Canary Wharf
London E14 4QA
Tel: 020 7425 8700
www.morganstanley.com/im/uk

Internet sites

www.londonstockexchange.co.uk	London Stock Exchange
www.nyse.com	New York Stock Exchange
www.nasdaq.com	NASDAQ Exchange
www.liffe.com	LIFFE/Euronext Exchange
www.investorschronicle.co.uk	Website of the *Investors Chronicle* magazine
www.prohpet.net	UK and US prices and charts
www.advfn.com	UK stock prices, research and charts
www.elitetrader.com	Trading information and discussion portal
www.gold-eagle.com	A good message board for precious metals
www.hoadley.net	Excellent free options software
www.numa.com	Trading and investment help
www.broker-advice.com	Find a good quality UK broker
www.equis.com	Home of Metastock charting software
www.finexprestel.com	End of day UK stock prices

Glossary

American style options – Options than can be exercised at any time during their life (See European Style Options).

At-the-money – Call and put option strikes that are nearest to the current price of the underlying.

Basis point (bp) – 0.01 per cent. For example, if an interest rate rises from 6 per cent to 6.5 per cent, it is said to have increased by 50 basis points.

Bearish – Bear, expecting prices to fall.

Bid – The price a prospective buyer is willing to pay for a security.

Bid–Ask spread – The difference between the bid price and the offer price, the best markets are where this differential is negligible. Be wary of markets that have a large bid–ask spread because they are very expensive to trade.

Bullish – Bull, expecting prices to rise.

Call option – An option contract that grants the buyer the right, but not the obligation, to buy a fixed amount of shares (in the case of stock options) at a set price (strike price) at or before a predetermined date (expiry). If the share fails to meet the strike price before the expiration date, the option expires worthless. You buy a call option if you think the share price of the underlying security will rise, or sell a call option if you think it will fall.

Call warrant – Confers the right but not the obligation to buy a quantity of an underlying asset at a predetermined price on or before a set date.

Cash settlement – A form of settlement whereby the underlying asset is not delivered to the holder of the warrant at expiry, but rather the holder receives the intrinsic value (if any) of the warrant in cash.

Contingent liability contract – A contract where one or both parties may have payment obligations in future in addition to the original contract costs. For example, futures and spread bets may require the purchaser to make payments in excess of their original investment if the markets move in an adverse way. In the case of warrants they have no contingent liabilities.

Cover – To sell a long position or buy back a short position as in 'I've covered my Vodafone position'.

Covered warrant – Covered warrants are a specific type of option where the contract is in the form of a tradable security. A third party, such as a bank, rather than the company in question, issues the security. The bank or issuer covers itself in the market.

Delta – The change in price of an option for evey one-point move in the price of the underlying security. A call option with a delta will increase by 50 points for every 100 points that the underlying rises and lose 50 points for every 100 that the underlying falls.

Derivative – Something that gets (derives) its value from something else. For example, an option to buy a common stock derives its value from the price of the underlying stock and is hence a derivative.

Diversification – The allocation of investment capital in a portfolio across different shares, sectors such as ETFs or regions in an effort to mitigate risk.

Dividend – A share of a company's earnings paid to each shareholder. Typically, dividends are paid bi-annually and are determined by the company's board of directors.

Dollar cost averaging – Investing equal amounts of money at regular intervals. Investing say £500 a month in a share is an example of dollar cost averaging. Theoretically, you will buy more shares when the price of your investment has declined, and fewer shares when the price has risen. This may lead to an overall cost basis that is lower than the average price per share.

EDSP – Exchange Delivery Settlement Price. All cash delivered futures contracts are expired against the EDSP.

ETF – A fund that tracks an index, but can be traded like a stock. Exchange Traded Funds consist of all the shares that are in the index with their relevant weightings. Most investors treat ETFs as simply a share that can be bought and sold short. They are gaining in popularity because they can give 100 per cent exposure to an index at far cheaper costs than trading a tracker fund sponsored by an institution.

European style options – Options that can only be exercised on the day of expire.

Ex-dividend – The date by which you must own a stock to receive its dividend payout. If you buy the shares on the ex-date, you buy without the right to the dividend. On the ex-date the shares will normally fall by a similar amount as the dividend paid out so there is no advantage or disadvantage by buying the shares on either day.

Ex-dividend date – The date at which buying the shares means that you won't be entitled to the dividend. These dates are all known beforehand.

Exercise – To invoke the right, which the warrant or option allows you to do, to buy or sell the underlying asset at the strike price or to receive the cash or share equivalent on settlement of the contract.

Filled – A completed order. A part fill would be, for example, when you're looking to buy 1000 shares but for whatever reason only bought 500.

Flat – Having no position (short or long).

Front month – The nearest month to expiry in a derivative contract.

Futures contract – A contract to buy or sell an amount of a commodity for a specific price at a specific point in the future.

GTC – An order to buy or sell a security that remains operative until the order is executed or cancelled. All orders unless instructed differently are normally cancelled at the close of the relevant market.

Hedging – Minimizing risk by being simultaneously long and short.

Hedge fund – Unregulated funds which primarily use aggressive trading strategies not allowed by more traditional vehicles such as unit trusts. Normally reserved for well capitalized and experienced investors. Most hedge funds are remunerated on a percentage of the profits, usually 20–30 per cent.

Historical volatility – Volatility averaged over a time period such as 10, 20 or 90 days.

Implied volatility – The volatility level that is implied by an option's price, takes into account historical volatility but also a view as to future volatility. It is therefore very possible for the levels of historical and implied volatility to differ dramatically.

In-the-money – Relates to options, all call strikes that are below the current price of the underlying are in-the-money. All put option strikes that are above the underlying are also in the money.

Intrinsic value – Relates to options. If the call option strike is below the current share price then the difference is known as the intrinsic value. Therefore all in-the-money options have an intrinsic value with out-of-the-money options having none, only what is know as time value.

ISAs – The individual savings accounts introduced in April 1999 by the UK government to replace Tessas and Peps.

Issuer – The party who must fulfil the obligations embodied in the warrant. For covered warrants the issuer is a bank, broker or investment bank.

LIBOR – London Interbank Offered Rate. The interest rate at which banks lend to each other.

Limit order – An order to buy or to sell a security at a specific price or better. Example: 'Buy 1000 shares of Vodafone at £1.20'. This would be placed when Vodafone is trading above £1.20 a share, and the purchaser is interested in waiting for a better price, and accepting the possibility that his preferred price will not ever be available, in which case the order will not be filled.

Liquidity – The amount of business done in a financial product or products. Where possible you always want to trade products that have good liquidity primarily because they are cheaper to trade due to tight bid–offer spreads.

Long position – Having bought, but not yet sold. A long position is entered with the aim of profiting from an increase in price. Refer also to short position.

Margin – The amount of money needed to deposit with your broker in order to fund a position. With margined products only a percentage of the nominal value has to be lodged in cash, normally between 5–20 per cent.

Market order – An order to buy or sell immediately at the best price available.

Mark to market – Adjust the value of an asset or liability to reflect the current market price.

Naked – Options that are sold on securities when the seller does not actually own shares of the underlying securities. For example, if you sold Bass call options without owning any stock then the short option position would be described as naked.

NAV – Net asset value. The price of each share of a fund. It is calculated by subtracting the fund's liabilities from its total assets, and then dividing that figure by the number of shares outstanding. The NAV is the amount of money that an investor would receive for each share if the fund sold all of its assets, paid off all of its debts and distributed the proceeds to the shareholders.

Noise – Normal everyday market movement, up and down without really going anywhere.

Offer/Ask – The price at which a prospective seller is willing to sell a security.

Open interest – The amount of open contracts in a futures market. Traders prefer to deal in markets with good open interest because it means plenty of liquidity.

Open position – A trading position long or short that has not been closed out.

OTC – 'Over the counter', a financial instrument that is not traded on an exchange. A currency transaction is an example.

Out-of-the-money – Relates to options. All call option strikes that are above the current underlying price are said to be out-of-the-money, and vice versa for puts.

Overbought – A term used to describe a market or a stock that has appreciated so rapidly and has generated such excessively bullish sentiment that a near-term decline is highly likely.

Oversold – A term used to describe a market or a stock that has declined so rapidly and has generated such excessively bearish sentiment that a near-term rally is highly likely.

PEPS – Personal Equity Plan, superseded by Individual Saving Accounts (ISAs).

Premium – The value of an option or warrant, if an option cost 80 points then the 80 is referred to as the option premium.

Put option – A put option is a contract that gives the buyer the right, but not the obligation to sell a stock (in the case of a stock option) at a predetermined price (strike price) at or before a predetermined date (expiry). Basically you would buy a put option if you think the stock will fall and sell a put option short if you think a stock will rise.

Resistance – The price at which a prior advance was terminated or a future advance is likely to terminate.

Risk adjusted return – A measure of how much risk a portfolio has employed to earn its returns.

Rollover – When a position in one month is transferred into another. For example a trader who rolls a long position over would normally sell the front month and buy the following month. Rollovers are normally carried out when the front month is about to expire.

SEC – US Securities and Exchange Commission, similar to the UK's FSA.

SIPPS – Self Invested Pension Fund, a personal pension that the owner can manage himself/herself.

Short position – Having sold, but not yet covered. A short position is entered with the aim of profiting from a price decline. When shares are sold short, the short seller borrows the stock in order to transact the sale. The position must eventually be covered by purchasing the stock in the market and returning it to the lender.

Slippage – Relates to stop losses and is the difference between where the stop loss price is and where the order was actually filled. If the order to sell 1000 BT at £2.00 on stop was filled at £1.99 then there is 1p of negative slippage.

Spread – The simultaneous purchase of one contract and the sell of another related contract. Buying gold, selling silver is an example of a spread trade, and the trader is doing this on the assumption that gold will out-perform silver in both a rising and falling market.

Stamp duty – Stamp duty is a government charge. In the UK the current levy is 0.5 per cent paid by the buyer on share transactions. In the case of covered warrants and other types of contract stamp duty is not payable.

Stop loss – A predetermined price at which a position will be closed to protect against further loss. The use of 'stop losses' is the only inherently reliable way for a trader to manage risk.

Strike price – All option contracts have a strike price which is the price that an option can be converted into shares (in the case of a stock option). A Vodafone £1.30 call option gives the holder the right to buy shares at £1.30 and this is the strike.

Support – The price at which a prior decline was terminated or a future decline is likely to terminate.

Tick or point size – The minimum amount that an instrument changes in price.

Time decay – Options and warrants are wasting assets, time decay measures the amount that an option/warrant will lose over a period of time.

Time value – The amount by which an option's premium exceeds its intrinsic value.

Trading range – A market where prices are range bound by a higher and lower price band. Normally markets will range trade when there is little or no news.

Unit trust – A fund that invests in a portfolio of shares and securities. Unit trusts are available on a full range of markets from the specialized, such as a trust that only invests in mining stocks, to index tracking funds. Unit trusts usually charge a fixed rate on assets under management.

US style options – Options that can be exercised at anytime until expiry.

Volatility – The degree of movement in the price of a stock or other security.

Warrant – A certificate, usually issued along with a bond or preferred stock, entitling the holder to buy a specific amount of securities at a specific price, usually above the current market price at the time of issuance, for an extended period, anywhere from a few years to forever. In the case that the price of the security rises to above that of the warrant's exercise price, then the investor can buy the security at the warrnt's exercise price and resell it for a profit. Otherwise, the warrant will simply expire or remain unused.

Write – Another word for selling short an option.

Yield – The percentage return on an investment.

Index